The WikiLeaks Paradigm

Stephen M. E. Marmura

The WikiLeaks Paradigm

Paradoxes and Revelations

palgrave
macmillan

Stephen M. E. Marmura
Department of Sociology
St. Francis Xavier University
Antigonish, NS, Canada

ISBN 978-3-319-97138-4   ISBN 978-3-319-97139-1   (eBook)
https://doi.org/10.1007/978-3-319-97139-1

Library of Congress Control Number: 2018952072

This Palgrave Pivot imprint is published by the registered company Springer Nature
Switzerland AG
The registered company address is: Gewerbestrasse 11, 6330 Cham, Switzerland

Acknowledgements

Work on this book project got seriously under way during a sabbatical in 2014–2015. I thank St. Francis University for providing me with this opportunity. As the work evolved I received support from various individuals. I am grateful to Peter Mallory and Laura Eramian for their constructive comments and advice on the book proposal. I also received useful feedback on several chapter drafts from Patricia Cormack and Peter Mallory. Elizabeth Marmura took the time to proofread the final draft, and this too was greatly appreciated. Additional advice and/or encouragement came from Lynda Harling-Stalker, Norine Verberg, Rod Bantjes, Riley Chisholm, John Phyne and David Lynes. Shaun Vigil at Palgrave Macmillan provided friendly guidance throughout the proposal and manuscript preparation process. So too did Glenn Ramirez during the final stages of manuscript preparation and submission. I benefitted greatly from the insights of three very knowledgeable anonymous reviewers who supplied feedback on the book proposal and sample chapters. The third reviewer also provided very helpful and supportive comments regarding the complete draft. My wife, Bridget Revell, and my children, Hana and Alex Marmura, provided love and support throughout this project. Further encouragement came from Heather Marmura, Timothy Marmura, E.J. Revell and A.J. Revell. I will always be grateful to my parents, Michael Marmura and Elizabeth Marmura, for helping to instil my lifelong love of learning and general fascination with the world around me.

CONTENTS

CHAPTER 1

Introduction: WikiLeaks as a New Form of Activism

Abstract As an electronic whistle-blower platform with global reach, WikiLeaks poses a unique challenge to state and commercial institutions. Yet, its efforts to galvanize the public have met with uneven success. To understand why, and to appreciate WikiLeaks' significance as an expression of counterpower, it is necessary to consider the informational and communicative paradoxes the group faces. These paradoxes must be examined in relation to the contingencies and longer-term political and economic trends affecting WikiLeaks' fortunes, and the shifting strategies the group has pursued over time. Attention to these matters provides insight into the nature of the networked, post-truth media environment and the challenges it poses to activists today.

Keywords Revelations • News • State power • Counterpower • Paradoxes

The whistle-blower platform and activist network known as WikiLeaks made its official appearance in 2006 with the registration of its website, *WikiLeaks.org*. Since that time, the organization and its charismatic leader, Julian Assange, have gained worldwide attention and remain the subject of intense political and academic controversy. While WikiLeaks was not the first player to leak state or corporate secrets to the public, the unprecedented scope and scale of its disclosures were guaranteed to earn the group

© The Author(s) 2018
S. M. E. Marmura, *The WikiLeaks Paradigm*,
https://doi.org/10.1007/978-3-319-97139-1_1

notoriety. That much was apparent during 2010 when WikiLeaks began publishing the contents of roughly 750,000 secret US military and diplomatic documents, passed to the organization by Private Bradley Manning who had obtained the material while serving with US forces in Iraq. Significantly, WikiLeaks sought and gained assistance in this endeavour from five leading international newspapers. The resulting disclosures, which led to calls for Assange to be arrested and charged under the US Espionage Act, included extensive records of large-scale civilian casualties at the hands of American forces. The drama surrounding the leaks reached its peak during "Cablegate", when Assange decided to release the remaining bulk of nearly 250,000 US diplomatic cables directly on *WikiLeaks. org*, for fear that the encrypted cache of documents was about to be compromised.

While WikiLeaks' prominence in the media faded for a time after Cablegate, the group did not remain idle. In 2013, it came to the defence of Edward Snowden when the former National Security Agency (NSA) officer leaked details of the massive US state surveillance programme known as PRISM. It also continued to leak information from a variety of sources, including proceedings from the pending global free trade agreement known as the Trans Pacific Partnership (TPP). WikiLeaks returned fully to the limelight with its phased release of emails belonging to the Democratic National Committee (DNC), during the eventful run-up to the US federal election of 2016. The leaked emails, which suggested a concerted effort within the DNC to marginalize the popular candidate Bernie Sanders, in turn triggered a cascade of conspiracy theories, countertheories and accusations of "fake news" advanced by political players and media pundits across the political spectrum. Inevitably, WikiLeaks itself came under fire, particularly from Democrats. The group was again accused of endangering national security, this time for allegedly colluding with Russia to subvert the US election process to the benefit of the Trump campaign.

WikiLeaks' abiding commitment to the ideals of "information freedom" and "radical transparency" continues to earn the organization the wrath of a growing collection of governments, financial institutions and corporations, even as it has spawned imitators. And the incidents referred to above suggest that debates about the group's enduring social and political significance are set to continue for many years to come. So far, thesubstance of these debates has ranged from legal and normative considerations to questions regarding WikiLeaks' character, novelty and effectiveness. To what extent are WikiLeaks' activities like or unlike those of other groups and individuals engaged in leaking information? Are Assange and company guilty of treason or should they instead be viewed as heroic champions of free speech? What challenges does WikiLeaks pose to increasingly distrusted mainstream news outlets? Insofar as any or all such lines of inquiry hold interest for social scientists it is often due to a larger underlying concern, namely, does the new form of activism WikiLeaks embodies represent a truly effective and expanding form of counterpower?

It was the development of a digitally enabled and highly interconnected global media environment that allowed for the type of activism WikiLeaks pioneered. At its most basic, WikiLeaks serves as an electronic drop-box for anonymous whistle-blowers wishing to pass along sensitive information. Its initial membership consisted largely of former hackers well versed in the art of encrypting and storing such information. Unlike the case for most activist groups, it is the skilled use of media technologies per se, as opposed to grassroots mobilization, which provides WikiLeaks with its chief means for challenging the status quo. By disclosing information jealously guarded by state institutions, banks, businesses or other powerful actors—but deemed by WikiLeaks' membership to belong within the public domain—the organization hopes to create an open media environment marked by radical transparency. In Assange's view, those institutions that prove able to adapt to this new situation will necessarily become more accountable and democratic in the process. Those unwilling or unable to do so will become increasingly rigid and secretive, ultimately undermining their legitimacy in the eyes of the citizenry.

The efficacy of the "WikiLeaks paradigm", namely, the organization's stated mission as a whistle-blower platform and its corresponding mode of activism, is considered here through reference to the trajectory of its overall career. Rather than focusing on the group's roots in hacktivist subculture or its internal politics, emphasis is placed instead on WikiLeaks' evolving tactics and strategies, particularly with respect to the major leaks and related political fallout referred to above. The objective is to identify the most important factors affecting WikiLeaks' mixed record of successes and failures in winning grassroots' support, steering public opinion, provoking political protest and influencing mainstream and alternative media discourse. It is only through mutual appraisal of the group's specific goals and attributes on the one hand, and the shifting and often confusing contexts in which it operates on the other, that both WikiLeaks' limitations as a journalistic enterprise and its unique but contingent ability to catalyse political change may be fully appreciated.

The larger argument of this book is that WikiLeaks' capacity to operate as an agent of social/political change in the US, while initially negligible, has increased over time and in a way that the group's opponents will find difficult to reverse. The factors at work in this regard are varied and include the changing nature of WikiLeaks' tactics and strategies, the vicissitudes of establishment politics in America and the increasing use of the organization's resources by a variety of grassroots "agitators" and/or niche media outlets. Critical as well is the influence of larger global and economic trends. It is important to consider how these work upon and interact with the factors listed above, and how they influence WikiLeaks' commitment to exposing wrongdoing at the systemic level and not merely within any one economic or political institution. Over the course of its career WikiLeaks has proven increasingly adept at negotiating a political and media landscape marked by growing distrust of dominant institutions, the proliferation of "truth markets" and alternative and mainstream expressions of conspiracy theorizing.

Chapters 2, 3 and 4 focus attention primarily on the challenges posed to WikiLeaks whenever it attempts to educate the public concerning information ostensibly withheld from it by powerful interests, but which arguably has a direct bearing on the well-being of ordinary citizens. Here, I contend that the obstacles confronting activist groups wishing to communicate with mass audiences today are at least as formidable as those that existed prior to the development of the World Wide Web. The web is frequently cited as a boon to social movements and other non-institutionalized political actors. Through an analysis of events surrounding Cablegate, and consideration of WikiLeaks' ambivalent relationship to mainstream news outlets, I demonstrate that the contemporary hybrid, that is, mass and new media environment, exacerbates and compounds many of the barriers to effective communication faced by those who challenged the political status quo during an earlier phase of capitalism. This reality holds profound implications for an organization dedicated to a purely informational mode of activism.

Chapters 5 and 6 address WikiLeaks' place within the American political and media landscape from a rather different angle. Here I maintain that WikiLeaks' ability to influence public opinion, and by extension the agendas of various grassroots activists and established political players, is greater than might at first appear to be the case. Many of the factors that worked against the group early on, including a heavy reliance on legacy news media and a lack of strong roots in American civil society, appear to have benefitted WikiLeaks over the longer term. The central argument of these chapters is that WikiLeaks has both contributed to and benefited from a crisis of legitimacy on the part of the US political establishment, itself tied to a global crisis of the nation state. WikiLeaks' ability to affect mainstream political and media discourse was clearly demonstrated following its disclosure of the DNC emails during the run-up to the federal election of 2016. However, the activist platform's potential to facilitate dissent is more deeply rooted in the broader crisis referred to above and in the organization's related capacity to tap into fears and issues of concern to a broad cross section of the public.

The chapters of this book may be read as independent analyses of various episodes in WikiLeaks' career. They take on greater significance, however, when considered together. As indicated above, WikiLeaks' evolving strategies have been shaped by larger economic and political trends. Hence, while the chapters draw on a range of theoretical perspectives pertaining to the specific issues at hand, the book is also informed by several overarching theoretical and substantive concerns. A sustained effort is made to situate WikiLeaks' activities within the broad context of what Manual Castells (1996) terms the global network society, and within what Jayson Harsin (2015) identifies as a neoliberal "regime of post-truth". Relevant ideas corresponding to both frameworks, along with the complementary ideas of other researchers and theorists are elaborated. Both contexts are highly relevant when contemplating the types of challenges WikiLeaks faces.

As the work of Castells (1996), Harvey (2005), Sassen (2014) and others makes clear, increasing economic globalization lies at the root of the present crisis of the nation state. For at least the past four decades, governments around the world have become progressively beholden to international monetary institutions and trade agreements, while proving unwilling or unable to resist the demands of transnational corporations and their domestic lobbies. One result is that citizens have become less trusting of politicians and less inclined to view them as representative of the popular will. WikiLeaks has become increasingly devoted to exposing the secrets of those who benefit most from this situation. It provides a valuable resource for groups and citizens dedicated to alternative visions of democracy and/ or who remain determined to resist the "new world order". Hence, as with the anti-globalization movement(s) with whom it often cooperates,

WikiLeaks now represents an expression of counterpower within the same digitally networked environment exploited by capital (Castells 2012). The crisis of the nation state in turn bears a direct relationship to the arrival of what Harsin (2015) and others describe as a post-truth cultural and media environment, one marked not only by growing distrust of political institutions but also by similar suspicion of "compromised" mainstream news organizations. One result has been a proliferation of alternative sources of information and opinion online, produced at low cost by grassroots organizations and citizens. Capitalism in its current "reflexive" phase has responded adeptly to this situation. Rather than producing mass commodities for mass markets, increasingly sophisticated attempts are made to locate or create consumer niche markets for which products may be customized. This requires relentless profiling vis-à-vis the surveillance of consumer behaviours such that tastes, preferences and lifestyle choices may be identified, and audiences targeted with the appropriate products and services (Andrejevic 2013). This logic extends to the identification of "truth markets". Personalized news products are tailored to compete with or co-opt the disparate political viewpoints expressed by countless consumers, citizens' groups, self-styled pundits and social movements. A key consequence for WikiLeaks is that it must strive to make itself heard within an increasingly crowded attention economy.

As the title of this book suggests, WikiLeaks' efforts to pursue its agenda are both revelatory and marked by paradoxes. They are revelatory in a dual sense. Most obviously, WikiLeaks is dedicated to exposing the secrets of powerful organizations to ordinary people. In addition, its efforts are revelatory in the way they shed light on the nature of a rapidly evolving media environment, and the way they reflect larger developments at the levels of grassroots activism and establishment politics. And WikiLeaks' experiences are paradoxical in ways that could only hold true for a group dedicated to disseminating information on such a vast scale. Nowhere was this more apparent than during the organization's early attempts to make leaked material available for public use. As Jacques Ellul (1965, 87) once observed, rather than being empowering, exposure to excessive amounts of information is often paralysing. It prevents rather than enables clear understanding and judgement. As explained in Chap. 2, this paradox lies at the crux of the communicative challenges confronting WikiLeaks.

Following Giri (2010), Zizek (2011) suggests that what is most radical about WikiLeaks, and what makes it so despised by the American political establishment, has less to do with the specific content of various leaked documents than with the challenge the organization presents to the formal functioning of power. Indeed, individuals such as Assange or NSA whistle-blower Edward Snowden stand out precisely because they have sidestepped the proscribed legal and institutionalized means for addressing official wrongdoing, choosing instead to speak directly to the public. However, this avoidance of conventional channels has only been partial, confronting WikiLeaks with another paradox. To better address a mass audience, Assange chose to avail his organization of what is still widely regarded as the most effective means for doing so, namely, through established mass media outlets. However, the resulting cooperation with large, mainstream news organizations has arguably compromised WikiLeaks' ability to elicit strong demands for meaningful political change from the public. It remains unclear, however, whether a viable alternative exists for any group attempting to challenge the status quo by revealing the secrets of the powerful.

"Objectivity" has been the dominant ideal guiding news reporting since the establishment of the journalistic profession (Schudson 2001). Assange champions a remarkably similar notion, "scientific journalism", as a means for overcoming problems of news bias frequently attributed to the mainstream press. The underlying idea is that the raw information journalists work with to produce a story is also made available to readers. Assange insisted on this when WikiLeaks chose to cooperate with the *New York Times*. In Chap. 2, I argue that this approach, while noble in principle, could never resolve the problems of mainstream news reporting Assange hoped it would address. The latter derive from prevailing structures of belief and interpretation, not a shortage of information. And there is little to suggest that exposure to countless alternative sources of "news" has produced a better informed or more politically engaged public. The audience fragmentation referred to above does not immunize citizens from the influence of dominant ideologies and top-down propaganda. Rather, as Jodi Dean (2002) contends, it may readily be harnessed to suit the requirements of "communicative capitalism" by encouraging pseudo-democratic forms of politics and activism online.

Today, virtually any social actor striving to become politically relevant or hoping to bring about widespread and enduring social change has little choice but to make use of new—that is, digitally based—media. However, when compared with activist groups or social movements that grew out of workers' associations, neighbourhood communities, ethnic enclaves or religious organizations, WikiLeaks' goals and methods appear particularly inseparable from the media it utilizes. WikiLeaks does not organize marches, gather petitions, knock on doors or hold meetings in church basements. Nonetheless, as Zizek (2011) recognizes, grassroots receptiveness to WikiLeaks' mission remains essential if the organization truly hopes to catalyse political change, and particularly change radical enough to "reach beyond the limits of representative democracy". The reason is straightforward. Leaks are deemed dangerous or undesirable by the institutions WikiLeaks targets primarily, although not always exclusively, due to their potential to provoke some form of public action or backlash. Without this implicit threat, the main targets of WikiLeaks' disclosures would have much less to fear.

These points relate to another paradox regarding WikiLeaks' agenda, one already hinted at. This concerns the organization's unprecedented and widely recognized accomplishments as an outlet for whistle-blowers on the one hand and its apparent inability to galvanize the public and trigger political protest in the manner its leadership desires on the other. As observers such as Fenster (2012, 800) and Uricchio (2014) have noted, this disjuncture appears most pronounced in the case of the US and was particularly glaring during the major leaks of 2010. This is a curious situation given that American diplomatic and military activities were the target of these widely publicized and sensational disclosures. Even when the actions of US officials or military personnel have been exposed as unethical, illegal or potentially at odds with American interests, there has been little visible reaction in terms of any widespread protest or social movement activity. It is intriguing to observe, however, that WikiLeaks has inspired such activity elsewhere. Perhaps most notably it played a small but arguably important role in the early Arab Spring uprisings of 2011, a point to be returned to shortly.

Collateral Murder is the title of a video disseminated by WikiLeaks online on April 5, 2010, primarily through YouTube. It has been hailed by some as the organization's most iconic act (Christensen 2014). The edited footage from which it was produced was delivered to Assange along with countless other classified documents, by Private Bradley Manning. The footage was taken from inside an Apache helicopter and displays the visual field of the two American pilots as they fire on unarmed Iraqi civilians, killing many including two Reuters' news cameramen in the process. By circulating the video online, WikiLeaks addressed the public in a seemingly elegant and effective manner. Rather than simply posting vast amounts of leaked military data, much of it largely incomprehensible without additional background information, the decision was made to highlight one particularly disturbing incident to drive home the brutality of US military operations in Iraq. The clear intent was to instil public outrage and ignite protest, thus putting pressure on the government to end an illegal war.

Despite the creativity and commitment of those who edited the video, and despite its startling content and wide circulation online, *Collateral Murder* did not provoke the reaction that WikiLeaks had hoped for. In fact, this was a key factor behind Assange's fateful decision to seek assistance from mainstream news outlets later that year (Dunn 2013). To better appreciate these matters, it is useful to contrast public reception to *Collateral Murder* in the US with WikiLeaks' positive involvement—in terms of inspiring political action—in the early Arab Spring uprisings of 2011. Such comparisons are important. While WikiLeaks may operate within a global media environment and while it may espouse a universal mission aimed at citizen empowerment, popular responses to its activities will necessarily be shaped at the national and regional levels. In Chap. 3, attention is given to the national, historic and media-related contingencies influencing public reactions to relevant leaks in each case. This includes examination of the role played by mainstream news institutions in both contexts, with *Al Jazeera*'s supportive role in relation to the Arab uprisings contrasted with the conservative discursive frameworks surrounding media coverage of *Collateral Murder* in the US.

The release of *Collateral Murder* was soon followed by publication of the Afghan War Logs on July 25, the Iraq War Logs on October 22 and the Cablegate leak on November 28 of 2010. As with Collateral Murder, all three leaks were associated with the same cache of 750,000 documents, then unprecedented in scope and volume, passed along to WikiLeaks by Bradley Manning—now Chelsea Manning—who obtained the material while serving in Iraq in 2007. In contrast to the earlier video release, the three major leaks named above were presented to the public with the cooperation of major international news organizations including the *New York Times, The Guardian* and *Der Spiegel*. In Chap. 4, I provide a content analysis of the first month of coverage of the Cablegate leak by the *New York Times*. It was this leak, drawn from over 250,000 secret US diplomatic cables, that more than any other earned WikiLeaks the wrath of the Obama administration, intensifying its efforts to have Assange extradited to the US to stand trial.

As countless political economy studies of news content make clear, the claim that the free, that is, corporate, news media serve as a reliable check on the official abuse of power, while not entirely baseless, cannot and does not deliver on such a promise. In general, mainstream news commentary reflects the perspectives of powerful interests while marginalizing alternative points of view. Sensitive or inconvenient facts or paths of journalistic investigation are regularly excluded, with the public exposed to only a limited range of media debate on issues that may directly affect them (Curran 2005; McChesney 2008). These points hold salience at a time when the ready availability of alternative source material for journalists online and/or competition from rivals such as WikiLeaks have been argued to facilitate greater freedom and willingness on the part of established news organizations to play their vaunted watchdog role. Such a role was not evident in relation to the *New York Times* coverage of Cablegate. Rather, in keeping with the critical political economy literature, and as highlighted in the case of leaks about Iran's alleged nuclear weapons programme, I demonstrate in Chap. 4 that the Cablegate material was utilized in a manner that kept relevant reporting and commentary squarely within the parameters of elite consensus and debate.

Chapter 5 is concerned with WikiLeaks' apparent success in surmounting at least some of the obstacles described in Chaps. 1, 2 and 3. Here, the organization's changing targets, including the security/surveillance state and pending free trade agreements, are considered in view of WikiLeaks' early experiences, Assange's anarchist philosophy and the growing prominence of conspiracy theorizing in America's political and media landscape. These issues are in turn linked to the global crisis of state legitimacy and to related anti-globalization social movement activity embodied in protest movements like Occupy. While acknowledging that WikiLeaks' concerns and activities overlap strongly with the latter, I emphasize that the group's influence extends even further. WikiLeaks now provides inspiration and resources to a range of activist groups across the political spectrum. Of special note, Assange's worldview and agenda find echoes within conspiracy-oriented media outlets in the US such as Alex Jones's popular *Info Wars* and *Prison Planet* websites, and more generally within the populist right.

Despite growing public distrust of mainstream news sources, most people continue to rely on familiar brands such as the *New York Times*, BBC World, FOX news, CNN, and so on, for most information they receive about the world. At the same time, and as emphasized above, alternative sources of information continue to proliferate, addressing the needs of more committed and/or partisan segments of the public and often serving as vehicles for the spread of unsubstantiated rumours and niche-oriented propaganda. I argue that on balance WikiLeaks has benefitted from both trends. Despite accusations of "selling out" from some quarters, its early cooperation with major news operations cemented the whistle-blower platform's reputation as a credible source of authentic, leaked information. This has allowed WikiLeaks to provide fodder for mainstream and alternative news forums alike, reinforcing partisan disputes and fuelling conspiracy theories, even while provoking further uncertainty about whom or what sources of authority may be trusted. Nonetheless, WikiLeaks remains vulnerable to the very dynamics it exploits. As Zizek (2011) observes, "The price one pays for engaging in the conspiratorial mode is to be treated according to its logic."

The importance of these points is underscored in the final chapter of the book, where attention is directed to the major news events preceding and immediately following the US federal election of 2016, with emphasis placed on WikiLeaks' role in the DNC email leak. As previously suggested, this leak took place within the context of a genuine crisis of public trust with respect to the two main political parties, itself the reflection of a larger global crisis of the state. Voter disgust with mainstream political candidates was palpable. Large numbers of voters looked to "alternative" candidates Bernie Sanders and Donald Trump, neither of whom received strong support within the upper ranks of their own parties. Ironically, though perhaps predictably, when the DNC leaks revealed attempts to marginalize Sanders, WikiLeaks gained new respect from some commentators on the political right, including Sean Hannity of FOX News. Meanwhile, many "progressives" accused the organization of conspiring with Russia to sabotage Hillary Clinton's bid for the presidency. The net result was even greater public disillusionment with the political establishment, an outcome arguably consistent with WikiLeaks' anarchist agenda.

The latter developments suggest that in some respects at least, the challenge to the political status quo posed by WikiLeaks may resist discipline or assimilation. Regardless of its questionable popularity with the public at large, WikiLeaks has arguably become a potent symbol of the times, tapping into widespread sources of anxiety and discontent. For these and other reasons it makes for a fascinating case study, one useful not only for considering the types of problems likely to confront activist organizations at the level of media representation, but also for appraising the larger contexts and shifting sets of circumstances that may serve to either facilitate or undermine the success of any social actor committed to political change. At a time when dominant forms of activism are themselves in transition, becoming ever more dependent upon the digital infrastructures of the global network society, a careful appraisal of the issues and paradoxes referred to above is clearly warranted. These will now be considered in turn, beginning with the dilemmas posed to WikiLeaks by the intersection of new and older modes of information dissemination and journalistic practice within an increasingly fragmented public sphere.

References

Andrejevic, Mark. 2013. *Infoglut: How Too Much Information Is Changing the Way We Think and Know.* New York/London: Routledge.
Castells, Manuel. 1996. *Rise of the Network Society.* Oxford: Wiley-Blackwell.
———. 2012. *Networks of Outrage and Hope.* Cambridge: Polity Press.
Christensen, Christian. 2014. WikiLeaks and the Afterlife of Collateral Murder. *International Journal of Communication* 8: 2593–2602. http://ijoc.org/index.php/ijoc/article/viewFile/3209/1243.
Curran, James. 2005. Mediations of Democracy. In *Mass Media and Society*, ed. James Curran and Michael Gurevitch, 122–149. London: Hodder Arnold.
Dean, Jodi. 2002. *Publicity's Secret: How Technoculture Capitalizes on Democracy.* Ithaca and London: Cornell University Press.
Dunn, Hopeton S. 2013. "Something Old, Something New...": WikiLeaks and the Collaborating Newspapers – Exploring the Limits of Conjoint Approaches to Political Exposure. In *Beyond WikiLeaks: Implications of Communications, Journalism and Society*, ed. Benedetta Brevini, Arne Hintz, and Patrick McCurdy, 85–100. New York: Palgrave Macmillan.
Ellul, Jacques. 1965. *Propaganda: The Formation of Men's Attitudes.* New York: Vintage Books.
Fenster, Mark. 2012. Disclosure's Effects: WikiLeaks and Transparency. *Iowa Law Review* 97: 753–807 https://ssrn.com/abstract=1797945.
Giri, Saroj. 2010. WikiLeaks Beyond Wikileaks? *Mute*, December. http://www.metamute.org/en/articles/WikiLeaks_beyond_WikiLeaks.
Harsin, Jayson. 2015. Regimes of Posttruth, Postpolitics, and Attention Economies. *Communication, Culture and Critique* ISSN: 1735-9129. http://onlinelibrary.wiley.com.libproxy.stfx.ca/doi/10.1111/cccr.12097/epdf.
Harvey, David. 2005. *A Brief History of Neoliberalism.* Oxford: Oxford University Press.
McChesney, Robert W. 2008. *The Political Economy of Media: Enduring Issues, Emerging Dilemmas.* New York: Monthly Review Press.

Sassen, Saskia. 2014. *Expulsions: Brutality and Complexity in the Global Economy.* Cambridge, MA: Harvard University Press.

Schudson, Michael. 2001. The Objectivity Norm in American Journalism. *Journalism* 2 (2): 149–170. http://journals.sagepub.com/doi/abs/10.1177/146488490100200201.

Uricchio, William. 2014. True Confessions: WikiLeaks, Contested Truths, and Narrative Containment. *International Journal of Communication* 8: 2567–2573. http://ijoc.org/index.php/ijoc/article/view/2770/1246.

Zizek, Slavoj. 2011. Good Manners in the Age of WikiLeaks. *London Review of Books* 33 (2): 9–10. https://www.lrb.co.uk/v33/n02/slavoj-zizek/good-manners-in-the-age-of-wikileaks.

CHAPTER 2

Information Abundance and Media Credibility in a Fragmented Public Sphere

Abstract WikiLeaks strives to inspire grassroots activism and facilitate political change by revealing the secrets of powerful interests. Its early strategies included recruiting citizens to interpret and distribute leaked information, and the pioneering of "scientific journalism". These efforts were plagued by problems of information overabundance and ultimately proved insufficient for countering the influence of dominant ideology on media discourse. WikiLeaks may address mass audiences by cooperating with major news organizations while sacrificing its radical agenda, or operate independently, preserving its mission while risking irrelevance. The dilemmas facing WikiLeaks are compounded due to the increasing fragmentation of the public sphere, and related attempts by industry to cultivate disparate "truth markets".

Keywords Information abundance • Activism • Journalism • Interpretation • Ideology • Truth markets

Considered from one angle, WikiLeaks appears emblematic of a new era, one marked by radical transparency and information abundance. This is because in addition to its impressive achievements as a whistle-blower platform the very mode of activism WikiLeaks embodies is inseparable from two more general and related developments. First, the advent of the World Wide Web put an end to the near monopoly formerly held by states and large corporations over the production and distribution of news and other forms of information to mass audiences or national publics. As Castells (2013) emphasizes, older processes of mass communication now coexist with the phenomenon of "mass self-communication", whereby countless individuals and groups express their opinions, share their worldviews and forge common projects online. Second, as state and commercial organizations have become increasingly dependent on computer networking technology, their capacity to conceal and safeguard information has been progressively undermined. In a context wherein virtually all major forms of communication and data storage are digitally interconnected, guaranteeing "information security" represents a monumental challenge.

Cleary, however, this picture is incomplete. Thanks to WikiLeaks, ordinary citizens do have access to a far greater number of sensitive documents than they had before. Yet, the sheer volume of information that might potentially be leaked vastly exceeds that which existed a mere generation ago. In proportionate terms, citizens now have access to less such information (Roberts 2011). Moreover, the obstacles facing any non-institutional actor hoping to address a given public or mass audience with its message remain formidable. Most people continue to rely on major news providers to gather and interpret information about the world they live in, and mainstream news is far more likely to reinforce than challenge the status quo. Likewise, the proliferation of digitally based niche media and alternative sources of news does not necessarily provide an antidote to the problems commonly associated with excessive top-down control of information on the part of state bureaucracies or media corporations. As the work of Dean (2002, 2009), Harsin (2015) and others suggests, such proliferation may deepen and extend as much as mitigate processes of ideological domination once associated with mass communication and an earlier phase of capitalism.

This chapter considers the types of obstacles these realities pose for WikiLeaks whenever it attempts to engage the American public, and by extension inspire citizens to work for social and political change. The obstacles in question are explored here at a general level, while Chaps. 3 and 4 consider their specific relevance to the cases of the Collateral Murder and Cablegate leaks, respectively. As indicated above, the main problems WikiLeaks faces stem from dynamics long associated with mass communication, but which now include additional informational and media dilemmas closely linked to capitalism in its present reflexive phase. Consequently, appreciating the often-paradoxical nature and general significance of the problems WikiLeaks confronts demands close attention to the evolving, networked character of the contemporary media environment. It also means reflecting on the ways in which WikiLeaks differs from most expressions of grassroots activism, and how these differences inform and condition the strategies it adopts.

This chapter builds on the premise that the most critical challenges WikiLeaks faces in the pursuit of its goals are communicative or representational in character. In other words, problems encountered by the organization in its efforts to manage and present information to the public in a way that inspires action. This premise might at first seem surprising, particularly since WikiLeaks faces major difficulties of another kind. I refer here to the considerable pressure the group has come under from state bodies and commercial enterprises determined to end to its activities. Ongoing efforts to undermine WikiLeaks have resulted in financial problems for the organization, and the harassment of core members and supporters. At the time of writing, the group's leader and public face, Julian Assange, remains in the Ecuadorian embassy in London where he was granted diplomatic immunity by the Ecuadorian government in 2012. While a United Nations legal panel asserted his right to travel freely in 2016, in the absence of any guarantees of immunity from the British authorities, Assange fears that if he leaves he will be extradited to the US to be prosecuted under the Espionage Act.

The rationale for a focus on issues pertaining to communication and media representation is straightforward, and relates to the points raised above. Despite the pressure it has come under, WikiLeaks has consistently proven able to safeguard and disseminate sensitive and ostensibly "scandalous" information while ensuring it receives widespread exposure. Consequently, the organization's ability or inability to inspire grassroots action or affect public attitudes must be understood not simply in terms of its capacity to make leaked information widely available. Even more critical is its ability to communicate effectively. Nonetheless, the fact that WikiLeaks' modus operandi makes ongoing harassment of the organization by powerful interests all but inevitable remains highly relevant. Insofar as it continues to incur the wrath of powerful institutions, any public sympathy for WikiLeaks or recognition of its virtues as a potential check on power necessarily hinges on the understanding that there is corruption to be exposed and dangerous secrets to be revealed.

Before proceeding further, it is important to acknowledge that "leaking", that is, surreptitiously passing along confidential information to the press, has a long history. It is therefore necessary to consider what if any-thing distinguishes WikiLeaks from others who engage in this activity. In general, leaking tends to be associated with two, sometimes overlapping, types of situations. These include muckraking and/or whistleblowing practices on the one hand, and cases related to political infighting, charac-ter assassination, smear campaigns, and so on, on the other. In the US, the term muckraking is largely synonymous with investigative reporting, par-ticularly that aimed at exposing illegal or unethical activity on the part of the powerful. Well-known examples from the Progressive Era, roughly the 1890s to 1920s, include the anti-racist editorials of black activist Ida B. Wells in *The Memphis Free Speech and Headlight*, and a series of featured pieces by Lincoln Steffens in *McClure's Magazine* that spotlighted wide-spread political corruption in American cities. A more recent example, and one which provided a valuable resource for Chap. 4 of this volume, is Gareth Porter's *Manufactured Crisis: The Untold Story of the Iran Nuclear Scare* (2014).

Such instances arguably constitute "journalism as activism", a practice which continues to evolve within the new media environment (Russell 2016). WikiLeaks clearly views itself as continuing in this tradition, one that has often been closely associated with whistleblowing on the part of organizational insiders dedicated to exposing various forms of wrongdo-ing. A noteworthy example concerns the largest pre-WikiLeaks disclosure of all. This occurred in 1971 when Daniel Ellsberg leaked the Pentagon Papers to the *New York Times*. The documents in question comprised a study revealing that successive US administrations had deliberately misled the public about their aims and activities in the Viet Nam war. Bradley Manning played a similar role to Ellsberg when he supplied the material leading to the major WikiLeaks disclosures of 2010. Another relevant example, one given further attention in Chap. 5, concerns the cooperation between National Security Agency operative Edward Snowden and jour-nalist Glenn Greenwald in exposing the mass state surveillance programme known as PRISM in 2013.

As previously indicated, leaking may also be deployed for less noble purposes, namely, to pursue personal vendettas or for use in smear cam-paigns, political attack ads, and so on. Unlike whistleblowing and activist journalism, such instances are motivated less by the desire to create a more just society, and more by an intent to discredit or demonize one's enemies or political opponents. Today, the term "doxing" (or "doxxing") is often used to refer to such activity when the information in question is gathered and disseminated entirely online. The latter term originates from "docs", itself short for documents (Fish and Follis 2016). The most important examples of this type of leaking with respect to the concerns of this book relate to the increasing prevalence of scandal politics in the US and elsewhere. As Castells (2013, 245) observes, over the last several decades American politics have been "largely dominated by the reports and counter-reports of scandals and damaging information directly aimed at political leaders or their proxies".

There can be little doubt that scandal politics is now a fully institutionalized aspect of political life in the US, where it is largely facilitated by those whom Castells (2013) refers to as "media hitmen". Castells (2013, 196–197) draws attention to a three-step process in this regard. First, the hitmen dig up dirt on a political target. The dirt is then given to pollsters who discover which pieces of information are most damaging in the minds of voters. Finally, the pollsters deliver their findings to political consultants who ensure that the two or three most damaging lines of material make their way into TV, radio and direct-mail pieces designed to destroy the reputations of opponents. One implication of such activity, together with the proliferation of non-professional news and information sources, is that the line separating "responsible journalism" from politically motivated scandal politics is often blurry. This reality has sometimes placed WikiLeaks in a vulnerable position. For example, many of WikiLeaks' more progressive critics now claim that the organization's disclosure of the Democratic National Committee (DNC) emails in 2016 was driven less by a desire to expose political corruption, and more by Assange's personal hostility towards Hillary Clinton.

In practice WikiLeaks is open to receiving material from virtually any source, with the proviso that the information in question is deemed authentic. It is the perceived journalistic value of leaked information rather than the specific motives of leakers that are of primary concern to the organization. Certainly, it is the case that any judgements regarding what information should be disclosed to the public necessarily reflect the goals, interests and value systems of those doing the disclosing. Of course, mainstream news organizations are no more value-neutral or disinterested in this regard than WikiLeaks or any other relevant player. For present purposes, when approaching WikiLeaks as a paradigm or model of activism, it is most useful to distinguish it from other individuals or groups engaged in leaking in three key respects: its dedication to providing a secure platform for leaked information from anonymous sources as its core activity, its related self-proclaimed status as a journalistic enterprise and the scope and scale of its social/political project. I address the last concern below.

Controlling access to in-house information has long been a preoccupation of large-scale institutions. So too has the parcelling out and "spinning" of selected messages for public consumption. Historically, in industrialized democracies like the US, such concerns gained urgency with the successive appearance of mass circulation newspapers, magazines, radio and television. Then, as now, access to and influence over the content of mass media outlets was relied upon by political parties, state bureaucracies and large businesses to provide the means for shaping their public image, and hence for presenting their goals and authority as commensurate with the popular will. As Jacques Ellul (1965, 121) once observed with respect to all modern democracies, "Propaganda is needed in the exercise of power for the simple reason that the masses have come to participate in political affairs." As an expression of counterpower, WikiLeaks was devised to undermine the dynamics associated with precisely this type of top-down information dissemination and control. Moreover, it attempts to do so at the level of society, whether conceived nationally or globally, and not merely with respect to any specific government, organization or institution.

While WikiLeaks may hope to subvert long-established dynamics of mass communication, it cannot fully escape their logic. This is because in fundamental respects the challenges it faces are no different than those confronting mainstream journalists, advertisers, political pundits, public relations specialists or any other actor striving to establish the content of their messages as worthy of public attention on the one hand, and as legitimate or credible on the other. However, for activist groups aiming to upset or transform the existing political order, these tasks are necessarily far more daunting than for those whose messages already resonate with pervasive common-sense frameworks derived from, and reinforcing, that same order. In other words, but far less obviously than in the case with most activist networks, WikiLeaks must do much more than simply present its audiences with "the truth". The point here is not that truth is purely relative in character, or that WikiLeaks' disclosures do not concern real events. Rather, it is to acknowledge that what people consider important or credible has as much to do with perceptions of the messenger, and with how information is interpreted and presented by the latter, as it does in any strict sense with objective "matters of fact".

It might at first appear that the content of WikiLeaks' disclosures does or should speak for itself. That while other activist networks must use creative rhetorical appeals to convince the public about the urgency of their programmes, WikiLeaks need only deploy its skills at acquiring, encrypting and disseminating information to advance its cause. As suggested above, however, this conclusion is unwarranted. The meaning or importance of any given piece of leaked information cannot be assumed to be self-evident. Furthermore, public understandings of relevant facts need not align with those held by WikiLeaks' membership. Consequently, if it truly hopes to provoke public outrage about hidden governmental or corporate activity WikiLeaks must ensure that the information it distributes is framed or conceptualized in an appropriate manner. Above all, it must demonstrate that non-transparent decision-making practices and related policy formation produce negative consequences for the citizenry. This task has proven far more difficult for WikiLeaks than its leadership initially anticipated. The multimodal and hybrid character of the media ecology in which the organization operates necessarily complicates the undertaking.

To begin, WikiLeaks must find ways to manage and organize the vast troves of data supplied to it by whistle-blowers. The trick is to do this in a manner which makes such information readily accessible and appealing as a resource for ordinary people. It bears emphasis that the documents provided to WikiLeaks by Private Manning in 2010, which include the combined material associated with the Afghan War Logs, Iraq War Logs and Cablegate leaks, number approximately 750,000. Perusing such material in its original, leaked condition is not an option for those who wish to view the documents first-hand. At the same time, organizing such information coherently represents a major undertaking. To this end, WikiLeaks has long encouraged public volunteers to sort through and arrange leaked material in a manner that allows those interested to locate specific types of content more easily. As Snickars (2014) observes, it is through such efforts that WikiLeaks most closely approximates the "wiki" ideal of collaborative content provision.

Two points deserve emphasis in this regard. First and as previously indicated, *WikiLeaks.org* was never intended to function solely as a clearinghouse for leaked information, but was also created to promote WikiLeaks' activist agenda. For this reason, its public leader Julian Assange provides political tracts and commentary on the site to help visitors appreciate the significance of WikiLeaks' disclosures. It should also be noted that the collaborative efforts referred to above necessarily constitute an interpretive endeavour, since they involve the formulation of criteria for categorizing and highlighting specific information. Second, and related to the first point, there was initially some faith on Assange's part that existing elements within civil society might serve as effective grassroots conduits, progressively sowing awareness within the public as to the need for greater transparency on the part of powerful institutions. Consequently, in addition to inviting citizen support in terms of organizing material within *WikiLeaks.org*, efforts were made to promote crowdsourcing and to encourage independent blogger/activists to further interpret and distribute leaked material.

It did not take long for Assange to abandon this strategy. As Lynch (2012) notes, an initial faith in the public's ability to analyse complex documents outside their direct experience set WikiLeaks apart from other crowdsourcing ventures such as Wikipedia. However, Assange soon became convinced that amateur bloggers lacked the requisite background knowledge to adequately contextualize relevant material (Fenster 2012). A related problem is also evident. WikiLeaks' diffuse membership of global volunteers and sympathizers represents neither a strong cross section of American society nor a well-defined constituency within it. Rather, it is comprised largely of elements closely associated with the same hacktivist subculture in which WikiLeaks has its roots. It was the latter, including those affiliated with the group Anonymous, who came to the aid of WikiLeaks in 2011 by launching distributed denial of service (DOS) attacks against corporations such as Paypal and Visa after the latter cut off services to WikiLeaks. While clearly valuable to WikiLeaks in terms of cyber-defence, these actors belong to a highly individualistic subculture largely committed to technical prowess and Internet freedom for its own sake (Milan 2013; Steinmetz and Gerber 2015). As such they appear ill-suited for inspiring grassroots action throughout mainstream American society.

The case of the hacktivist subculture cited above and the important matter of its relative insularity from major sectors of the American public is itself symptomatic of a more general trend. As researchers such as Castells (1997) and Dahlgren and Gurevitch (2005) have documented, the rise of a neoliberal global economy has been paralleled by a decline in the traditional institutions of civil society, particularly those once associated with organized labour and traditional party politics. These changes have been pronounced in the US, where a reduced social welfare role for the state has led to increasing demands for more local, community-based decision-making on the one hand and the growth of non-localized net-works of individuals and groups sharing similar interests, goals and ideals on the other. The common thread is that less state commitment to the collective public good has encouraged an ethic of autonomy on the part of self-identified communities and networks, and hence to a related rise of single-issue politics (Bimber 2003). These changes have in turn been accompanied by an increasing proliferation of identity-based media, and hence a more fragmented public sphere.

It is now widely recognized that the Internet provides the ideal medium for facilitating "homophily", or the tendency of like-minded individuals to gravitate together (Wilhelm 2000). I draw attention to this issue here for two reasons. First, identity-based social media platforms are generally ill-suited for addressing a mass public, at least in the American context. In cases where new media do appear to have played a key role in this regard, as well as in inspiring widespread social protest—for example, during the early Arab Spring uprisings of 2011—both the broader media environ-ment and prevailing social/political conditions were very different than those obtaining in the US. This issue will be given closer attention in the next chapter. Second, the Internet's amenability to the creation of social networks based on such criteria as religious affiliation, sexual orientation, ethnicity, political outlook or connection to some aspect of popular cul-ture is increasingly being exploited by commerce in a manner which argu-ably forestalls effective political mobilization. More will be said on the last point later in this chapter.

The realities touched on above clearly influenced Assange's eventual decision to collaborate with major international news media outlets in 2010. This move bore fruit when the *New York Times, The Guardian* and *Der Spiegel* released the Afghan War Logs on July 25 and the Iraq War Logs on October 22 of that year. Together, these leaks entailed the publi-cation of nearly 500,000 documents chronicling multiple aspects of the two post-9/11 wars. Soon afterward, WikiLeaks and its "media partners" began publishing the first of the Cablegate leaks. This development is given attention in Chap. 4. However, some of the factors informing Assange's decision to cooperate with the mainstream news media deserve mention here. For example, the portion of the public that actively visits *WikiLeaks.org* is marginal. Fuchs (2014, 2727) observes that the *New York Times* ranks #121 in the list of the world's most accessed websites, with *The Guardian* listed at #146 and *Der Spiegel* at #177. By contrast *WikiLeaks. org* stands at #12,267. These figures fit with a larger picture in which the top 7% of websites take over 80% of overall traffic in the US. The top ten outlets, all of which are traditional news providers or major online portals, account for 25% of market share (Brevini and Murdock 2013).

It might be objected that even the readership of the *New York Times* amounts to only a small, relatively elite segment of American society. However, as Herman and Chomsky (1988) emphasize, the influence of this and other large "agenda-setting" news organizations extends well beyond their immediate readership or viewership by providing a model for smaller news organizations to emulate. Furthermore, most news outlets belong to large media monopolies or even larger conglomerates, the convergent interests of which are reflected in the ideological content of their products. It is for these reasons that Assange's decision to cooperate with the *Times* requires scrutiny. On the one hand, by teaming up with this major online newspaper Assange achieved two important goals for the organization he leads. He guaranteed that the information leaked by Manning would receive international media attention, including extensive coverage within the US. And he established WikiLeaks' credibility as a reliable source of authentic leaked information. Critically, however, by providing large news operations with leaked material, Assange necessarily abnegated his editorial role.

These developments raise the question of how Assange felt he could avoid the trap of ideological co-optation. While this might be a non-issue with respect to reporting within *WikiLeaks.org*, dealing with it effectively while providing material to legacy media like the *Times* arguably represents a formidable if not insurmountable challenge. Two strategies appear to have informed Assange's thinking on this count. The first is frequently referred to by Assange in his writings and during interviews, and concerns his claim to be pioneering a new and more socially responsible form of journalism. Specifically, Assange promotes what he terms "scientific journalism" as a means for grounding and legitimizing the interpretive dimension of news reporting, thus establishing an effective antidote to the dangers of media spin (Lynch 2012). Simply put, scientific journalism means providing readers with direct online access to the same source material that journalists draw upon when putting together a news story. If relevant news coverage seems misleading or off the mark, or if reported facts appear to be stacked in a biased manner, then readers may consult the original data and judge for themselves whether the coverage in question appears fair.

Assange contends that over the long term, this approach will set a new and higher standard for journalism more broadly. Credibility will come to hinge on the provision of original source material with the major news media held more accountable to the public as a result. In fact, however, what is most striking about this approach is not its novelty, but rather the degree to which it mimics a strategy long pursued by journalists to resolve essentially the same problem. The latter concerns the controversial notion of "objectivity", which, as Schudson (2001, 162) emphasizes, has been the dominant guiding ideal of news reporting since journalism was first professionalized in 1922–1923. It was once considered natural that any given news operation reflected the political viewpoint of its owner. And when the market still allowed for genuine competition among newspapers espousing competing points of view, open media partisanship represented a democratizing force. As McChesney (2008, 91) points out, during the Progressive Era, it was not only "mainstream", that is, business-oriented, newspapers which thrived and multiplied, but also publications associated with the labour movement and socialist causes. However, with an increasing concentration of media ownership, and the buying or squeezing out of competition, such diversity would not endure.

A growing problem for newspaper owners during the late nineteenth and early twentieth century was that with the rise of media monopolies, the undisguised partisanship and polemic tone which had come to characterize news reporting began to look increasingly unfair and anti-democratic (McChesney 2008, 86–87). Pressure to change the style of news delivery had other sources as well. For example, the growth of mass circulation newspapers beginning in the mid-1800s meant a greater dependence on advertisers. A more neutral tone in political reporting was preferred by the latter, who wished to capture the largest possible—that is, bipartisan— audience of consumers. For these reasons, newspaper owners felt the need to encourage a form of journalism which appeared even-handed in its approach to such matters as electoral contests and differences in the policy positions adopted by the major parties (McChesney 2008, 29–30). Furthermore, reporters themselves felt threatened by competition from a burgeoning public relations industry. Those paid to sell the virtues of corporate or government policies were widely regarded by journalists as lacking a strong sense of public responsibility or due regard for the truth for its own sake (Schudson 2003, 162). To distinguish themselves from these "propagandists", journalists adopted the purist position that events should be reported exactly as they occur, undistorted by the subjective feelings or opinions of reporters.

Of considerable importance here, the journalistic pursuit of objectivity has itself been identified as a potential source of news bias (McChesney 2008, 30–34). The reason is not that journalists deliberately set out to mislead the public, or that they do not make genuine attempts to report fairly and honestly. Rather, a commitment to neutrality and objectivity, in conjunction with established news gathering routines and an institutional dependence on amicable relations with essential sources, necessarily skews reporting. Above all, claims and pronouncements emanating from the halls of power are repeated endlessly in the news media to the exclusion of other perspectives. In the absence of serious media critique, and/or sufficient background information, the public has little to draw upon in terms of assessing the veracity of what is being stated (McChesney 2008, 99–103). The potentially negative consequences of this dynamic are apparent when considering the political rhetoric that invariably precedes major military engagements. Grave assertions about the atrocities or crimes of a declared enemy are often repeated ad nauseam by politicians, establishment experts and media pundits. If or when the same claims are exposed as half-truths or debunked entirely, this typically occurs only after hostilities are well under way and the public's attention has been directed elsewhere.

It is the public's need for meaningful points of reference when appraising news content that scientific journalism was meant to address. Yet, by providing only objective facts in the form of "raw" leaked information this approach necessarily leads full circle back to the fraught issues of selection and interpretation associated with traditional reporting. It is highly unlikely that casual newspaper readers will appraise the merit of individual stories through reference to source material provided by WikiLeaks or anyone else. Rather, journalists are expected to interpret such material for them. And despite their purported commitment to objectivity, news outlets do play an active interpretive role vis-à-vis editorializing, analyses, punditry, and so on, in addition to organizing regular news reports in terms of familiar narrative structures (Schudson 2003, chap. 10). Ironically, given the nature of Assange's attempts to overcome media bias, to the extent that major news outlets are trusted to provide such interpretation, this is largely due to their relatively strong track record in terms of relating "objective facts", that is, figures, statistics, the statements of politicians, and so on, accurately.

The above points should be held in mind when considering a second strategy implicit in Assange's decision to cooperate with the major news corporations. This entails exploiting the very fact of the leaks as a source of rhetorical power (Fenster 2012). As noted earlier, *WikiLeaks.org* was never intended to serve only as a secure repository for leaked information, but also to advance WikiLeaks' social/political agenda. To a considerable extent, the goals of greater information freedom and radical transparency that the organization champions appear compatible with the democratic ideals ostensibly held by most Americans (Fenster 2012, 782). At the very least, participatory democracy requires at least some degree of transparency on the part of the state and/or with respect to the activities of elite pressure groups that influence government policies. In principle, therefore, it should be possible to deliver a major moral shock to the public simply by revealing the sheer scope and scale of the secret, and hence undemocratic, undertakings of the powerful.

When attempting to draw attention to what he regards as the main impediments to genuine democracy, Assange (2006) refers to the notion of "conspiracy as governance", an idea that receives further attention in Chap. 5. At its most basic, the concept refers to a reality wherein decisions holding profound implications for ordinary peoples' lives are increasingly made by powerful interests behind closed doors. The media strategy alluded to above fits with this general understanding. As Lievrouw (2014, 2639) observes, accountability from WikiLeaks' perspective, "is only possible when authority is confronted with huge and incontrovertible stocks of evidence that interconnect to create a total, systematic picture of wrongdoing or exploitation". By this logic, journalists may be trusted to provide the necessary background details pertaining to any given piece of leaked information, since the very magnitude of the disclosures provides the perceptual vantage point from which to appreciate their true significance. The conspiratorial nature of the governing order is put on full display, even as the inherent vulnerability of a system which cannot safeguard its deepest secrets is revealed. An outraged public is thus encouraged to act and demand change.

The fatal flaw in this strategy is that there is no inherent reason why the decision-making practices which Assange views as conspiratorial should be deemed problematic by most citizens. As public intellectual Walter Lippmann (1922) argued almost a century ago, the very complexity of modern democracies may limit the feasibility of governmental consultations with the public on all matters. The logical corollary to this argument is that identifying the most effective means for resolving many important issues is best left to the experts. As will be demonstrated in Chap. 4, this mindset informs the editorial line adopted by the *New York Times* with respect to Cablegate, where US diplomats receive repeated praise for executing their technocratic functions in the service of the state so effectively. To the degree that such "common-sense" discourse predominates in the media, Assange is less likely to come across as some sort of information Robin Hood than he is to be viewed as an irresponsible if not dangerous public menace. The critical point here is that regardless of whether WikiLeaks' revelations are presented piecemeal or in the form of a major scandal, their radical potential may readily be neutralized via routine news framing practices.

It is of course important to tread carefully here. The act of introducing secret or confidential information into the public domain on the scale of the Afghan War Logs, Iraq War Logs and Cablegate was clearly unprecedented, and as I will argue in Chap. 4, it was not without significant consequences. Nonetheless, it does seem clear that for such acts to have the desired impact on the public imagination, neither the provision of raw information nor the shock delivered by the magnitude of any given disclosure will suffice. Rather, the content and larger potential significance of leaked information must be linked, creatively, explicitly and repeatedly to threats to democratic life considered meaningful by large segments of the public. There is no shortage of potential targets in this regard. Examples include the backroom dealing behind major bank bailouts, the influence of powerful lobbies on Capitol Hill, the expansion of the security state to include routine mass surveillance, the creation of secret courts and extrajudicial killings post-9/11, America's apparent commitment to perpetual global war, and so on. WikiLeaks' problems in this area derive not from a lack of media attention to its disclosures, but rather from the reluctance of mainstream news organizations to make the necessary connections to such issues in a sufficiently adversarial or critical manner.

The discussion so far suggests that WikiLeaks remains in a classic catch-22 situation. Assange and his colleagues may promote whatever views they like on *WikiLeaks.org*, but only those already sharing the organization's outlook are likely to pay much attention. In the case of mainstream news reporting the problem is reversed. As countless studies dealing with the political economy of the mass media have demonstrated, deep or sustained critique of the social/political status quo is virtually non-existent in mainstream news commentary and for a very basic reason. As large, profit-seeking enterprises regulated by the state, news corporations are too deeply embedded in existing relations of power to bite the hand that feeds them. Furthermore, they have little incentive to do so since they share the same broad economic and political interests as other major commercial institutions. These realities tend to be masked by the fact that rigorous debate is ever-present in the media. However, as Herman and Chomsky (1988) emphasize, most such debate stays well within proscribed boundaries corresponding to disagreements amongst powerful elites, mirrored in disputes between the two main political parties, while alternative points of view and lines of argument tend to remain marginalized.

It is worth digressing to consider the way these realities are reflected at the level of public opinion and popular sentiment before turning to the issue of how competition from new online information sources, including WikiLeaks, fits into the larger picture. It is now a commonplace within communication studies that audiences do not consist of "cultural dopes" readily susceptible to whatever directives or ideas those in power choose to feed them. Instead, media audiences are better understood as constituted by self-conscious, reflexive agents capable of resisting dominant interpretations of reality. Information circulating in the media is actively engaged with and/or reinterpreted from the subjective standpoints of members of the public, or publics, characterized by important differences along the lines of race, religion, income, gender, sexual orientation, and so on. However, an important caveat is also in order. If people are to "resist" media messages in any politically meaningful sense, they require both the will and the resources to assess those messages critically. People cannot evaluate facts that they have never heard or read about, and they cannot deploy alternative frameworks of analysis or draw upon background knowledge with which they have no familiarity.

If one can accept the basic proposition that all societies partake of a dominant outlook or worldview, then the character and effectiveness of what Ellul (1965) once termed "integration propaganda" becomes far less mysterious. The citizen/consumer of the modern nation state is no more brainwashed or deluded in his or her beliefs than the members of earlier, or non-industrialized societies. However, he or she has been socialized in a very different manner. As Ellul (1965) emphasizes, the rise of propaganda and its centrality to practices of mass communication was closely linked to the industrial revolution and related processes of modern state-building. The latter entailed the mobilization of large populations uprooted from what was previously a rural and largely insular existence.

Overcoming the loss of identity and accompanying sense of anomie associated with this upheaval demanded new ideological frames of reference better suited to life within an otherwise alienating mass society. The latter included ideals of democratic participation, the work ethic, "freedom", individual success, the pursuit of happiness and the myth of progress, along with a more general identification with the state as a source of collective national identity and citizenship.

For the most part, these new doctrines and cultural points of reference did not arise primarily from within the uprooted populace. Rather, they were instilled through processes of socialization unique to modern states. Put differently, the importance of the socializing role played by mass communication increased in direct proportion to the disintegration of community as experienced by humanity throughout most of history. Premodern empires may have been vast, but life in the communities held within them was still largely defined by what Emile Durkheim called "mechanical solidarity", namely, socialization facilitated and maintained through face-to-face interaction and lifelong engagement with religious/legal and cultural/economic institutions deeply imbedded in local community life. By contrast, members of modern societies necessarily place their trust in abstract systems associated with state bureaucracies and impersonal market forces (Giddens 1991). And when communities no longer produce for themselves, people must be conditioned to address their increasingly manufactured and diversified needs as consumers. Likewise, the myths and stories people are raised on are derived less from the family, church or other institutions grounded in the immediate lifeworld, and are increasingly derived from profit-seeking entities representative of what Horkheimer and Adorno (2002) famously referred to in the 1940s as the culture industry.

None of this means that the public does not consist of reflexive agents who actively interpret what they read and hear in the media. For the most part, however, these interpretations and differences in outlook are held and contested within a broader cultural framework of widely shared and deeply internalized values, assumptions, attitudes and myths, themselves continually reinforced within the existing educational and media systems. Hence, as Stuart Hall (1984) argued in his famous essay *Encoding/Decoding*, even when specific messages about such things as the economy, gender roles, race, justice, and so on, are resisted or reinterpreted from the standpoints of different individuals or groups in society, this tends to occur in a such a way that deeply ingrained common-sense assumptions and ideological points of reference are left unexamined. Liberal feminists attempt to gain more equal treatment and workplace justice for women without attending to the structural bases of class inequalities. Christian conservatives complain about hedonism and "Hollywood values" while praising the same capitalist system responsible for the excesses of consumer culture. Self-proclaimed environmentalists shop for "green products". Those fighting for gay rights in the armed forces implicitly condone America's outsized global military presence, and so on.

Certainly, cases exist where those challenging dominant political/cultural assumptions do adopt genuinely "oppositional codes", alternative systems of meaning more universal in scope. For example, while most people associated with the LGBTQ community appear to favour same-sex marriage, some reject it because it is perceived to reinforce an unjust patriarchal system within which institutionalized marriage represents a key foundation. Likewise, some fighting for greater workers' rights believe that capitalism must be completely abolished rather than merely regulated. As Hall (1984) makes clear, however, such cases remain the exception. It is "negotiated" or partial expressions of opposition to dominant understandings of reality, such as those referred to above, that predominate in modern societies, and which ultimately serve to legitimize the larger system which accommodates them. Moreover, tastes and lifestyle preferences may be catered to through the production of appropriate commodities. Significantly, and as underscored in much of the cultural studies literature, this includes the co-optation and commodification of youth rebellion and other grassroots expressions of political dissent.

In general, people are less likely to question the veracity of media messages concerning subjects about which they have no strong opinions or with which they have little direct experience (Newton 2006; Wilhelm 2000). Similarly, when messages reinforce an existing attitude or bias, they are apt to be accepted, even when based on spurious information. Taken together these tendencies help account for the potency of wartime propaganda, an issue that receives attention in the next two chapters. By contrast, when individuals are confronted with messages that conflict with their values or existing understandings of reality, they tend to experience psychological discomfort or "cognitive dissonance" and are more inclined to reject them (Newton 2006). These points relate back to the issue of homophily cited earlier, and to the related tendency of people to seek out media which cater to their specific interests and/or which reflect their preexisting beliefs. While people's freedom in this regard has increased exponentially through use of the web, homophily has also been actively encouraged and exploited under the conditions of neoliberalism.

Thanks to industry's rapidly expanding capacity to gather and analyse the "big data" generated by citizen/consumers during such activities as web-surfing, credit card use, cell phone use, commuting, and so on, increasingly fine-tuned commodities may be produced to suit the tastes of ever-more demographics and consumer types. WikiLeaks must therefore compete for the public's attention within a context where self-constituted issue-publics, already narrow in their goals and outlook, are becoming further fragmented, their activities redirected to promote commerce. These developments suggest that there is more to the exploitation of homophily online than the mere promotion of specific news sites or social media platforms. As ever, the larger strategy of capital is to prefigure and contain all spheres of human cultural and political activity. Jodi Dean (2009, 2) captures this reality through reference to "communicative capitalism", which she defines as "the materialization of ideals of inclusion and participation in information, entertainment, and communication technologies in ways that capture resistance and intensify global capitalism".

In a similar vein, Harsin (2015) maintains that neoliberalism has brought with it a new "regime of truth", or in this case "regime of post-truth" (ROPT). This regime extends beyond the purely economic realm to include a larger strategy of governance and social control. Harsin works from Foucault's premise that all societies partake of a regime or general politics of truth in which certain forms of discourse, with their corresponding reality claims and means for producing knowledge, gain prominence and circulate in a manner commensurate with the functioning of dominant apparatuses of power. In the case of what Foucault termed "disciplinary societies", roughly corresponding to the mass societies referred to above, a relatively small number of dominant economic, political and media institutions work in complementary fashion to establish the conditions and set the parameters to produce authoritative truth claims and what is considered legitimate knowledge. Today, however, with the proliferation of digital technology and an accompanying reconfiguration of the relationship between state and economy—an issue explored more closely in Chap. 5—we are witnessing "a breakdown of the fiduciary status of truth-telling and confirmation/judgement and coordination in a so-called regime" (Harsin 2015, 329).

As Harsin's comments suggest, the post-war period of Keynesian or welfare capitalism was marked by a different truth regime than that associated with neoliberalism. Significantly, it corresponded to what Daniel Hallin (2000) refers to as the heyday of professional journalism with its accompanying ideals of objective reporting. Hallin (2000, 221) describes that period as one marked by a general belief in "progress, rationality and universal truths or standards, as well as a conviction that it is possible to be part of the 'establishment', with wealth, access and prestige, and simultaneously independent – an avant-garde in art, watchdog in the media". By contrast, under the ROPT, the respect once accorded to objective facts as the necessary building blocks for more comprehensive understandings of reality has been downgraded. Rather than trusting what is empirically verifiable, citizens are instead urged to "go with their gut". As Andrejevic (2013) suggests, this means that truth claims circulating in the media today are likely to be rejected or accepted at a visceral level, one amenable to pure conviction and absent of the doubts produced from weighing endless competing facts.

Today, the news apparatus increasingly takes the form of a "many-headed hydra" with competing truth markets identified and targeted within an affectively charged attention economy (Harsin 2015, 329). Related to this trend, a Gallup Poll conducted in 2016 found that Americans' trust and confidence in the mass media "to report the news fully, accurately and fairly" has dropped to its lowest level since 1972, with only 32% saying they have a great deal or fair amount of trust in the media (Swift 2016). Paradoxically, however, this lack of trust need not diminish the mainstream news media's hegemonic role in terms of shaping popular understandings of reality. This is because the increasing fragmentation of civil society into competing issue-publics and niche media markets guarantees that no single source of information or verifier/debunker of truth claims will ever emerge as definitive (Harsin 2015). Hence, no alternative information source can challenge the mainstream news media's dominant status. Consequently, recognized brands such as CNN, the *New York Times*, FOX, MSNBC, and so on, will almost certainly endure as the public's primary default sources of news, despite growing scepticism about traditional sources of information. At the same time, these media giants, along with any emerging competitors, will increasingly target specific audiences, each of which will perceive their favoured outlets as more credible than the rest.

It is important to recognize that under the conditions of neoliberal or reflexive capitalism, the consumer aggregates identified by marketers need not correspond to self-aware social collectives. Rather, as Andrejevic (2013, 42–50) observes, they are located and/or created through processes of "predictive analytics" and "sentiment analysis", made possible by

mining the data generated online through countless acts of social networking, tweeting, blogging, and so on. Harsin (2015) stresses the relevance of this development to the case of competing truth markets. He
contends that the latter must be understood as fundamentally different in
character than the self-organizing, reflexive publics and counterpublics
described by other researchers dealing with civil society and new media,
even while the same "truths" may circulate between them. Moreover, a
corresponding mindset is inculcated amongst members of the citizenry.
People are now conditioned to accept the reality that there is ultimately no
way to verify truth claims, to believe the truth arbiters in their own markets, and subsequently to engage in vigorous practices of counterclaiming
and debunking with those who disagree with them (Harsin 2015, 6). The
result is that citizens are effectively demobilized, left to engage in what is
essentially a semblance of democratic participation.

With these points in mind it is worth reflecting on the fact that despite
the relative paucity of visitors to its website, WikiLeaks has fared very well
on Twitter. Lynch (2014, 2679) notes that during a spike in its popularity
in 2011 WikiLeaks gained over a million followers, becoming only the
436th user of the service to do so. And in August 2016, at the height of
the DNC email scandal, WikiLeaks ranked fourth among non-profit organizations on Twitter with 5.49 million followers (Topnonprofits 2016).
Such success comports well with a media environment that includes millions of channels, websites and social media feeds, one wherein news is no
longer delivered or broadcast at regular intervals but rather "is composed
of millions of beeps and vibrations, revolving tickers that shape-shift and/
or disappear by the second" (Harsin 2015, 329). However, WikiLeaks'
successful exploitation of Twitter also brings one back to the same dilemma
outlined earlier, namely, the need to contextualize leaked information in a
manner which encourages critical thinking and allows for meaningful
political engagement. To the extent that they take the form of free floating
entities increasingly difficult to separate from misinformation, hoaxes or
rumour, "hard facts", leaked or otherwise, arguably lose their potential for
citizen empowerment, even as they provide fodder for rampant speculation and conspiracy theorizing.

Harsin (2015) emphasizes that under the present ROPT it is not only
ideologies, discourses and human bodies, but attention itself that is
increasingly managed. This reality, itself largely a response to increasing
market saturation, is best understood as a further elaboration of the ideological logic cited earlier with respect to Hall's work, rather than as

post-hegemonic. As Dean (2009) makes clear, the relentless demands now placed on the individual to forge and express a unique identity, "participate", be seen, network, market himself or herself, and so on, lie at the very heart of neoliberal ideology. The related undermining of any stable cultural points of reference that might give such activity lasting meaning is simultaneously assured when new consumer needs must continually be manufactured, and ever-more aspects of human activity predicted and modelled in advance. The ROPT thus represents the most recent manifestation of ongoing attempts by capital not only to commodify grassroots expressions of culture, but also to co-opt any related expressions of resistance to the existing economic and political order. As such, it is "ultimately designed to block the emergence of more inclusive social justice agendas or even the reorganization of political agency itself" (Harsin 2015, 332).

Today, politicians vie for public allegiance largely by exploiting "wedge issues". Emotionally charged topics like abortion, gun control, same-sex marriage, and so on, are addressed in a manner geared to agitate and divide the voting public, even as attention is diverted from such fundamental problems as deepening socio-economic inequality or the creeping consolidation of the security state. By the same token, an ongoing commitment to neoliberal economics and enhanced homeland security has become a matter of bipartisan consensus. The unspoken implication is that policies guaranteed to promote vast disparities of wealth are best accompanied by enhanced means for monitoring the population and suppressing dissent. In like fashion, internal and external threats—for example, Islamist terrorism, drug cartels, radical protest movements, "environmental extremism", and so on—can always be counted on to justify foreign wars or restrict civil rights at home. As previously emphasized, it is precisely such "conspiratorial" realities that WikiLeaks must link effectively to the content of its disclosures. Otherwise, the information scandals it facilitates may do little more than feed into the "managed spectacle of sharing, liking, debunking, and refuting 'issues'" referred to by Harsin (2015, 6).

The developments described above must be kept in perspective. Differences of political, religious and ideological outlook in the US are real, and as in any society they may never be entirely neutralized or co-opted. Furthermore, there are aspects of the trends and dynamics considered here that work to WikiLeaks' advantage. These matters are explored in Chaps. 5 and 6, where the DNC email and Russiagate scandals of 2016/17 are considered within the context of a growing political legitimation crisis. Nonetheless, it is also clear that the contemporary media environment presents formidable challenges for WikiLeaks whenever the latter strives to capture the imagination of the American public. Moreover, the group's reliance on a purely informational mode of activism and its close identification with journalism make it inherently more vulnerable to the problems of media representation addressed in this chapter than is likely to be the case for activist organizations with a stronger presence in civil society. The importance of these realities will be explored further in the next two chapters, with reference to WikiLeaks' release of the *Collateral Murder* video on YouTube, and the related Cablegate disclosures of 2010/11.

REFERENCES

Andrejevic, Mark. 2013. *Infoglut: How Too Much Information Is Changing the Way We Think and Know*. New York/London: Routledge.

Assange, Julian. 2006. Conspiracy as Governance. *me @ iq.org*: 1–4. http://naka-motoinstitute.org/static/docs/julian-assange-conspiracies.pdf.

Bimber, Bruce. 2003. *Information and American Democracy*. Cambridge: Cambridge University Press.

Brevini, Benedetta, and Graham Murdock. 2013. In *Beyond WikiLeaks: Implications of Communications, Journalism and Society*, ed. Benedetta Brevini, Arne Hintz, and Patrick McCurdy, 35–55. New York: Palgrave Macmillan.

Castells, Manuel. 1997. *The Power of Identity*. Oxford: Wiley-Blackwell.

———. 2013. *Communication Power*. 2nd ed. Oxford: Oxford University Press.

Dahlgren, Peter, and Michael Gurevitch. 2005. Political Communication in a Changing World. In *Mass Media and Society*, ed. James Curran and Michael Gurevitch, 375–393. London: Hodder Arnold.

Dean, Jodi. 2002. *Publicity's Secret: How Technoculture Capitalizes on Democracy*. Ithaca/London: Cornell University Press.

———. 2009. *Democracy and Other Neoliberal Fantasies: Communicative Capitalism and Left Politics*. Durham/London: Duke University Press.

Ellul, Jacques. 1965. *Propaganda: The Formation of Men's Attitudes*. New York: Vintage Books.

Fenster, Mark. 2012. Disclosure's Effects: WikiLeaks and Transparency. *Iowa Law Review* 97: 753–807. https://ssrn.com/abstract=1797945.

Fish, Adam, and Luca Follis. 2016. Gagged and Doxed: Hacktivism's Self-Incrimination Complex. *International Journal of Communication* 10: 3281–3300. http://ijoc.org/index.php/ijoc/article/view/5386/1707.

Fuchs, Christian. 2014. WikiLeaks and the Critique of the Political Economy. *International Journal of Communication* 8: 2718–2732. http://fuchs.uti.at/wp-content/IJOCWL.pdf.

Giddens, Anthony. 1991. *The Consequences of Modernity*. Cambridge: Polity Press.

Hall, Stuart. 1984. Encoding, Decoding. In *Culture, Media, Language*, ed. Stuart Hall, Dorothy Hobson, Andrew Lowe, and Paul Willis, 128–139. London: Hutchinson.

Hallin, Daniel. 2000. Commercialism and Professionalism in the American News Media. In *Mass Media and Society*, ed. James Curran and Michael Gurevitch, 218–237. London: Hodder Arnold.

Harsin, Jayson. 2015. Regimes of Posttruth, Postpolitics, and Attention Economies. *Communication, Culture and Critique* ISSN: 1735-9129. http://onlinelibrary.wiley.com.libproxy.stfx.ca/doi/10.1111/cccr.12097/epdf.

Herman, Edward S., and Noam Chomsky. 1988. *Manufacturing Consent: The Political Economy of the Mass Media*. New York: Pantheon Books.

Horkheimer, Max, and Theodor W. Adorno. 2002. *Dialectic of Enlightenment: Philosophical Fragments*. Trans. Edmund Jephcott. Stanford: Stanford University Press.

Lievrouw, Leah A. 2014. WikiLeaks and the Shifting Terrain of Knowledge Authority. *International Journal of Communication* 8: 2631–2645. http://ijoc.org/index.php/ijoc/article/view/2667/1240.

Lippmann, Walter. 1922. *Public Opinion*. New York: Harcourt, Brace and Company.

Lynch, Lisa. 2012. "That's Not Leaking, It's Pure Editorial": WikiLeaks, Scientific Journalism, and Journalistic Expertise. *The Canadian Journal of Media Studies* (Fall): 40–67. http://cjms.fims.uwo.ca/issues/special/Lynch.pdf.

Lynch, Lisa. 2014. "Oh, WikiLeaks, I would so love to RT you:" WikiLeaks, Twitter, and Information Activism. *International Journal of Communication* 8: 2679–2692. http://ijoc.org/index.php/ijoc/article/viewFile/2665/1236.

McChesney, Robert W. 2008. *The Political Economy of Media: Enduring Issues, Emerging Dilemmas*. New York: Monthly Review Press.

Milan, Stefania. 2013. WikiLeaks, Anonymous and the Exercises of Individuality: Protesting in the Cloud. In *Beyond WikiLeaks: Implications of Communications, Journalism and Society*, ed. Benedetta Brevini, Arne Hintz, and Patrick McCurdy, 85–100. New York: Palgrave Macmillan.

Newton, Kenneth. 2006. May the Weak Force Be with You: The Power of the Mass Media in Modern Politics. *European Journal of Research* 45: 209–234. http://onlinelibrary.wiley.com/doi/10.1111/j.1475-6765.2006.00296.x/full.

Porter, Gareth. 2014. *Manufactured Crisis: The Untold Story of the Iran Nuclear Scare*. Charlottesville: Just World Books.

Roberts, Alasdair. 2011. The WikiLeaks Illusion. *The Wilson Quarterly* (Summer).

Russell, Adrienne. 2016. *Journalism as Activism: Recoding Media Power*. Cambridge: Polity Press.

Schudson, Michael. 2001. The Objectivity Norm in American Journalism. *Journalism* 2 (2): 149–170. http://journals.sagepub.com/doi/abs/10.1177/146488490100200201.

————. 2003. *The Sociology of News*. New York: W. W. Norton & Company.

Snickars, Pelle. 2014. Himalaya of Data. *International Journal of Communication* 8:2666–2678. http://pellesnickars.se/wordpress/wp-content/uploads/2014/09/int_journal_communication_snickars_wikileaks1.pdf.

Steinmetz, Kevin F., and Jurg Gerber. 2015. Hacking the State: Hackers, Technology, Control, Resistance, and the State. In *The Routledge International Handbook of the Crimes of the Powerful*. New York: Routledge.

Swift, Art. 2016. Americans' Trust in Mass Media Sinks to New Low. *Gallup News*, September 14. http://news.gallup.com/poll/195542/americans-trust-mass-media-sinks-new-low.aspx.

Topnonprofits. 2016. Top Nonprofits on Twitter. August. https://topnonprofits.com/lists/top-nonprofits-on-twitter/.

Wilhelm, Anthony G. 2000. *Democracy in the Digital Age*. New York: Routledge.

CHAPTER 3

Lessons from *Collateral Murder*

Abstract The video *Collateral Murder* was released by WikiLeaks on YouTube in April 2010. It drew public attention to American atrocities in Iraq. Reception of the video by the American popular and news media is contrasted with WikiLeaks' modest contributions to the Arab Spring uprisings. WikiLeaks' activities were greeted positively in Tunisia and beyond, both by Arab activists and by the leading regional news network *Al Jazeera*. By contrast, *Collateral Murder* did little to galvanize the American public, an outcome largely attributable to its coverage by the US news establishment. Ultimately the US media's treatment of *Collateral Murder* served to strengthen popularized myths and mainstream rhetoric supportive of the status quo.

Keywords *Collateral Murder* • Imagery • Arab uprisings • *Al Jazeera* • American media • Myths

On April 5, 2010, WikiLeaks' published a video online entitled *Collateral Murder*. Its content was shocking, at least from the perspective of WikiLeaks' activists and presumably many others. It displayed footage taken from within an American Apache helicopter during an airstrike in Iraq in 2007. The pilots can be heard commenting callously as they fire on a group of civilians. When a passing van stops to help evacuate the wounded, the driver and vehicle are fired upon as well. At least 23 people

© The Author(s) 2018
S. M. E. Marmura, *The WikiLeaks Paradigm*,
https://doi.org/10.1007/978-3-319-97139-1_3

were killed in the attack, including the van driver, whose two young children inside the vehicle were badly wounded from the helicopter's cannon fire (Christensen 2014). A Reuters' news photographer and his driver were also among the dead. Unsurprisingly, the video contradicted the official military account of the same incident. According to the latter, American soldiers had been conducting a raid when they were hit by small-arms fire and rocket-propelled grenades. Reinforcements, including attack helicopters, were then called in, with the two Reuters' employees and "nine insurgents" killed during the fighting which allegedly ensued (Wing 2013).

An immediate source of embarrassment to the US political and military establishments, *Collateral Murder* quickly became the subject of intense media attention. Initially, Assange and the video's co-producers held high hopes that its release would provoke public outrage and lead significant numbers of US citizens to protest their government's actions and policies in Iraq (Dunn 2013). Americans were increasingly unhappy about the war, and relevant precedents had already been set. For example, the first US led attack on Iraq in 1991 was accompanied by large anti-war demonstrations, albeit grossly underreported by most American news outlets, in cities across the country. And on February 15, 2003, large-scale protest marches against the next looming invasion took place in over 600 cities worldwide. Decades earlier, during the Viet Nam war, dramatic media images depicting civilian victims of US aggression had served as potent catalysts for anti-war mobilization. Yet, despite *Collateral Murder*'s disturbing content and the high expectations of its creators, its release had little discernible effect in terms of rallying public opposition to the ongoing US military presence in Iraq.

The use of visual imagery to deliver a moral shock or jolt to public consciousness is nothing new. It is a tactic that has been deployed with varying degrees of success by activist groups for many decades. Greenpeace's use of media "mind bombs" during the 1970s to spark public outrage about such matters as whale hunting or the slaughter of baby seals is a classic example. In the case of WikiLeaks, the strengths and limitations of such methods are evident when contrasting the organization's modest role in the early Arab Spring uprisings with the more negative response to WikiLeaks' activities in the US. Comparison of these scenarios will be made here to draw attention to the importance of larger social and political realities in conditioning how activist messages are understood and hence responded to by various publics. This will in turn allow for greater insight into the more specific role played by the mainstream media in terms of shaping the political climate and influencing relevant perceptions and attitudes in both the US and Arab contexts.

Close attention to the role of the media is critical for a better appreciation of the American public's subdued response to *Collateral Murder*. It is equally important for understanding the initial success of the mass uprisings in Tunisia and Egypt. While the factors at work in each case were myriad, several stand out as particularly important. First, in the case of the Arab world, an initial spark for major protests was provided by a specific shocking event, knowledge of which spread rapidly through social media. At least as importantly and quite remarkably, a highly influential news organization, *Al Jazeera* (AJ), reported on relevant events sympathetically and in a fashion that complemented the media tactics of protesters. Rather than being subjected to what Lee (2014) terms "the protest paradigm", whereby mainstream media portray activists as violent, troublesome or quixotic, the satellite news agency provided protesters with moral and even technical support. WikiLeaks' modest contributions on the protesters' behalf fit seamlessly within this larger scenario.

By contrast, in the case of *Collateral Murder*, the video's positive reception by anti-war activists was not echoed in the mainstream media. Given that the video dealt directly with US military involvement in post-9/11 Iraq, it was perhaps inevitable that mainstream news reporters, official spokespersons and media pundits alike would draw upon the conceptual frames of homeland security and the Global War on Terror as their default points of reference for the provision of relevant commentary and debate. Clearly, deliberate or reflexive reliance on such frames necessarily limits the way even a highly disturbing visual text such as *Collateral Murder* is likely to be understood by the public. It essentially negates any perceived need for critique of US goals and policies in the Middle East or elsewhere. Worse still, at least from an activist perspective, when critical attention to the systemic bases of social problems such as war or human rights abuses are lacking, "scandals" such as *Collateral Murder* may end up reinforcing, rather than undermining, myths and ideological frameworks supportive of the status quo.

Before elaborating further along the lines indicated above, several matters concerning the nature and content of the WikiLeaks video require attention. First, it should be emphasized that *Collateral Murder* is more than simply a segment of leaked video footage. The piece was edited by Julian Assange, Birgitta Jonsdottir and other activists with the intent of creating a vivid and effective piece of anti-war propaganda, but one that also remained true to Assange's commitment to scientific journalism. Consistent with this commitment, both the original footage and the edited video were made available on a special WikiLeaks webpage so that viewers might judge the merits of the edited version for themselves. These edits include the video's title, limiting the footage to 17 minutes, and the provision of scripted introductory and closing commentary. The latter includes reference to the "relaxed atmosphere" visible amongst those about to come under helicopter cannon fire, along with sympathetic descriptions of some of those killed. There is also acknowledgement of the possibility that a few of the victims might be armed. Finally, some segments that contradict the official account of events are slowed down or replayed.

Predictably, these edits drew criticism from various government and military sources, as well as from mainstream news commentators. Bill Keller of the *New York Times* complained that the video "didn't call attention to an Iraqi who was toting a rocket-propelled grenade and packaged the manipulated event under the tendentious rubric 'collateral murder'" (Keller 2011). However, as Benkler (2013) observes, the opening slide of the edited video points to the possibility that the man in question was carrying a weapon. And as Assange (2010) explained during an interview on *Al Jazeera English*, the video's title was chosen due to the visible targeting of one of the victims, later identified as Reuters' employee Saeed Chmagh, who was lying wounded, unarmed and isolated on the ground. This was a clear war crime. Other critics, including comedian Stephen Colbert, chastised Assange for the more general sin of stepping out of correct journalistic bounds to create a video that was "pure editorial" (see Lynch 2013). Such criticism is worthy of note, particularly when recalling Assange's hope that adherence to the practice of scientific journalism would resolve the issue of establishing news credibility once and for all.

It is important to note both the timing of the video's release and the fact that *Collateral Murder* represented WikiLeaks' first major attempt to galvanize the American public. Published after a series of smaller leaks dealing with such matters as secret Scientology religious documents, political corruption in Kenya and money laundering by Icelandic banks, the video was released shortly before the vast disclosures associated with the material passed to WikiLeaks by Manning, namely, the Afghan War Logs, Iraq War Logs and those pertaining to Cablegate. The latter were publicized in cooperation with major news organizations in July, October and

November/December 2010, respectively. The failure of *Collateral Murder* to inspire widespread anti-war activism was a key factor behind Assange's decision to share these leaks with mainstream news outlets (Dunn 2013). As emphasized in Chap. 2, Assange felt that such cooperation was necessary to better engage a mass audience.

Collateral Murder has received praise as well as criticism, with many activists and intellectuals insisting that the video represented a major accomplishment. Zizek (2013, 256) contends that while US military operations may receive attention in the media, references to the type of situation captured in the video tend to be made only obliquely and in a manner that makes them easy to ignore. Similarly, Christensen (2014) notes that while one may read endless accounts of the brutality of war, few engender the type of feeling experienced when watching non-combatants being shot down by helicopter cannon fire. These assertions seem particularly apt when one considers the sheer magnitude of disclosures such as the Iraq War Logs, the cache from which the *Collateral Murder* footage was drawn. The cache consists of nearly 400,000 documents, chronicling multiple dimensions of the Iraq war from January 1, 2004, to December 31, 2009. They include records of thousands of unreported deaths, many involving US army killings of civilians. Yet, the Iraq War Logs never gained the notoriety of *Collateral Murder* and as Christensen (2014) suggests, it is the latter which will likely endure as the more iconic WikiLeaks product.

The issues of media reception and critique are complicated in this instance by the phenomenon referred to earlier as communicative capitalism. This is the term developed by Jodi Dean (2002) to refer to the means through which democratic ideals and aspirations are co-opted to suit the requirements of neoliberalism. According to Dean (2009, 17), contemporary practices of social media use by activists have been encouraged and harnessed by industry in a manner whereby the "proliferation, distribution, acceleration and intensification of communicative access and opportunity produce a deadlocked democracy incapable of serving as a forum for progressive political and economic change". In the case of anti-war demonstrations against the US invasion of Iraq, Dean's point is not that such protest was lacking, or that there were not many progressive anti-war media outlets offering meaningful critique of the Bush administration's policies. The problem was that these messages "morphed into so much circulating content, just like all other cultural effluvia flowing through communicative capitalism's disintegrated spectacles" (Dean 2009, 20).

These points relate to the larger problem identified in Chap. 2 concerning the balkanization of society into issue-publics and online communities increasingly exploited by capital in the form of truth markets. In the case of US military involvement in Iraq, anti-war messages circulated primarily in a media sphere that remained demarcated from those utilized by other identities operating online, as well as from the dominant news media. This is not to say that *Collateral Murder* was ignored, but simply to assert that in each sphere, different discursive practices and frames of reference were and remain dominant. For example, the video did receive attention on websites and news shows associated with the populist right. The intent, however, was mainly to demonstrate the propaganda aspects of the video and denigrate the efforts of anti-war activists. Likewise, while the "self-evident" brutality and injustice of *Collateral Murder* may have been clearly perceived and articulated in left-wing protest circles, its reception by the mainstream media was more ambiguous.

Cases whereby photographic images, news stories, online videos, information leaks, rumours, and so on, may serve to turn the tide of public opinion or mobilize protest with respect to a given issue are best regarded as exceptional. Moreover, any such instances will inevitably emerge from a highly contingent mix of social and political circumstances, and related technological affordances. Potential triggers for protest and dissent will necessarily vary across social and historic contexts. What might be regarded as inflammatory or outrageous within one setting may be viewed very differently or receive scant notice in another. These points are worth holding in mind not only when reflecting on the weak public response to *Collateral Murder* in America, but also when considering WikiLeaks' limited, but noteworthy role in the Arab Spring uprisings of 2011. To provide greater insight on these matters, attention will now be devoted to the Arab context before returning to the case of *Collateral Murder*.

It is now widely accepted that the primary causes of the Arab Spring were rooted in decades-old sources of popular discontent. Most Arab countries were and remain authoritarian in character, with democratic institutions either absent or poorly developed. In the cases of Tunisia and Egypt, where the first and most comprehensive upheavals occurred, political opposition had long been suppressed with elections geared primarily to maintaining systems of one-party rule. In both countries, the existing regimes were propped up by Western states, particularly the US, but also France in the case of Tunisia. And in both cases, these outside powers did little to encourage democratic reform. Additionally, the aid these powers provided was conditional and a source of public discontent. This was most obvious in the case of Egypt. The massive US financial and military assistance the country has received since 1979 remains contingent upon the maintenance of its domestically unpopular peace arrangements with Israel. Although ostensibly geared to end such activity, in practice these arrangements left Israel free to continue colonizing Palestinian land.

Above all, the economies in both Tunisia and Egypt were stagnant and government corruption was rampant. As in much of the region, few decent work opportunities existed to meet the needs of an increasingly youthful and rapidly expanding population. Compounding these problems, freedom of expression had long been severely restricted. Most of the major media outlets in countries throughout the Middle East and North Africa (MENA) fell under direct state control. Serious criticism of government policies by journalists, whether associated with state-owned or independent news operations, could mean loss of employment or even jail time. Significantly, however, in the decade preceding the uprisings, state control over the media had begun to be seriously challenged throughout the region.

Two related developments stand out in this regard. The first concerns the spreading use of the Internet, cell phones and related social media platforms within sizable segments of the population in much of the MENA region, particularly among relatively well-educated but largely unemployed urban youth. As Castells (2012) notes, it was this segment of the public which comprised the core of the uprisings in Tunisia, Egypt and beyond. And as Howard and Hussain (2011, 46) have shown, social media played a key role in the uprisings by providing this demographic with the "digital scaffolding" needed for the effective mobilization of civil society. The second, related factor pertains to the launch of the AJ news network in Qatar in 1996, and its rapid rise to prominence throughout the Arab world. In fact, as underscored by Marc Lynch (2012) and Howard and Hussain (2013), the two developments worked synergistically. Taken together they played a key role in the uprisings, both by preparing the groundwork for effective civil action and through the facilitation of a common Arab public sphere which transcended state boundaries.

Crucially, the arrival of the satellite news network AJ provided the basis for the emergence of a genuinely pan-Arab public sphere (El-Nawawy and Iskander 2003; Lynch 2006, 2012). Controversial subject matter that had long been barred from media forums by ruling elites, including government corruption, the influence of foreign powers on local economic policies, the unwillingness or inability of Arab governments to effectively back the Palestinian cause, the role of religion in politics and various aspects of women's and minority rights, were now given air time on a regular basis. The network also gave the impetus to competition from other emerging networks, thus raising public expectations with respect to greater openness in media content more generally (Lynch 2012). Moreover, as suggested above, a new youth culture marked by a more critical attitude towards state authority was further enhanced through the spreading use of new media platforms like Facebook, YouTube and Twitter. In authoritarian states marked by extensive internal security apparatus and harsh restrictions on freedom of assembly, social media allowed citizens to identify common concerns, debate key issues and devise strategies of civil disobedience (Howard and Hussein 2013).

It is against this backdrop that WikiLeaks made its own contributions to the Arab Spring. It is important to acknowledge that while WikiLeaks did contribute to the growing anger felt by Arab citizens throughout the MENA region in identifiable ways, it did not provide the initial trigger for political mobilization. The latter, widely credited with sparking the first uprisings in Tunisia, involved the self-immolation of a 26-year-old Tunisian street vendor named Mohamed Bouazizi (Lynch 2012). It should be emphasized that the circumstances leading to Bouazizi's death were hardly unique, and that the incident resonated with ordinary people not only in Tunisia, but across the Arab world. Ultimately, Bouazizi's unintended martyrdom highlighted the vast disparities of wealth and opportunity, and the arbitrary exercise of power familiar to citizens throughout MENA.

Bouazizi was a resident of Sidi Bouzid, a town in central Tunisia. Its long history of labour unrest and violent anti-government protests made Sidi Bouzid much like other peripheral towns and cities across the country (Lynch 2012, 70). Mohamed Bouazizi was a labour activist who had supported his mother and siblings since childhood by selling produce on the street-side from his fruit cart. Earning a meagre income, he was often forced to pay bribes to avoid having his cart confiscated by the police. On December 17, 2010, Bouazizi tried to avoid paying an inspector's fine, appealing first to police and then to the municipal authorities. At each attempt he was physically beaten by security officials (Howard and Hussain 2013, 18). Intensely frustrated by the public humiliation he had suffered, and by ongoing experiences of police corruption and abuse, Bouazizi doused himself in gasoline and set himself ablaze outside the local municipal building.

In a matter of hours, hundreds of friends and sympathetic youth, many of whom had also suffered at the hands of local authorities, were protesting at the site. Mohamed's cousin Ali recorded the initial protest and distributed the video online. In the coming days and weeks, similar protests erupted across the country with Tunisians demanding regime change. On January 14, two days after the head of the armed forces refused to open fire on protesters, Tunisian President Ben Ali and his family fled to Saudi Arabia for asylum. Audiences around the Arab world watched the drama unfold on television, even as the protests spread beyond Tunisia. Copy-cat suicides occurred in Egypt, and on that country's annual "police day" massive protests began against police and government corruption. As the Egyptian protests grew, and the final days of the Mubarak regime approached, AJ became an increasingly important source of information and inspiration to the Arab masses. Its coverage made it apparent to Arabs everywhere that "the unthinkable was actually happening" (Castells 2012, 60).

While WikiLeaks did not provide the impetus for mass political mobilization in the Arab world, it did contribute to the uprisings in two key respects. First, it leaked information concerning government corruption in Tunisia, as well as information concerning other politically charged issues of interest to Arabs more generally. Second, and related to the above, WikiLeaks provided a model which was emulated both by local activists and by AJ. In both respects, the release of documents associated with Cablegate produced effects which were contingent upon other developments in Tunisia and the wider region (York 2013, 229). Of note, WikiLeaks partnered with the homegrown activist website *Nawaat.org*, giving it exclusive rights to numerous Tunisia-related cables. The leaks were then translated into French for the benefit of the reading public and put on a special website called TuniLeaks, where they were accompanied by contextualizing commentary. They were available for viewing less than an hour after WikiLeaks published the cables on its own site on November 28 (York 2013, 230).

The TuniLeaks website dealt primarily with corruption on the part of Ben Ali and his extended family. As York (2013, 229) points out, the leaked information did not tell Tunisians anything new, but provided solid confirmation of what they already believed or suspected. The leaks reinforced the growing public anger that finally exploded following Bouazizi's tragic death several weeks later. One important consequence of TuniLeaks' activity was that it made it more difficult for France and the US to continue their open support for the Ben Ali regime. WikiLeaks also contributed to growing Arab discontent by providing information about such matters as governmental and police corruption in Egypt. Other Cablegate transcripts highlighted the subservience of various Arab governments to Western interests (Saleh 2013). Not least, Cablegate revealed that while Arab leaders regularly paid lip service to the Palestinian cause, an issue close to the hearts of Arabs throughout MENA, Palestinian national and human rights were in fact low on their list or priorities.

WikiLeaks also inspired AJ to set up a "transparency unit" dedicated to receiving leaks from anonymous whistle-blowers. In fact, the news organization was soon responsible for a major leak of its own. Between the 23rd and 26th of January 2011, AJ released the "Palestine Papers", nearly 17,000 leaked documents detailing the inner workings of the US-sponsored Israeli/Palestinian peace process from 1999 to 2010. The news organization followed Assange's lead vis-à-vis scientific journalism, making the complete cache of documents available on their website along with extensive commentary and background information. It also shared the leaked documents with the *Guardian*. In terms of its political importance, the leak revealed the lengths to which the Palestinian Authority was willing to go to accommodate Israeli and US demands, even to the point of sacrificing Palestinian rights guaranteed in international law. The incident has received relatively little scholarly attention, coming as it did between the first protests in Tunisia and the outbreak of even larger uprisings in Egypt. However, as York (2013, 229) points out, it represented a milestone in Arab news reporting, being the first time a well-known Arab news outlet had played a major whistleblowing role since 1986 when the Lebanese paper *Al-Shiraa* exposed the Iran-Contra Affair.

The discussion above makes clear that WikiLeaks' contributions to the Arab Spring uprisings must be appreciated against the backdrop of the larger transformations then sweeping the region. Crucially, the social/political context in which leaked information both inspired and was utilized by relevant players in the Arab world was very different than the US context during roughly the same timeframe. In the case of MENA, while people were angry about the worsening circumstances with which they had been struggling for decades, they were also both hopeful and relatively united with respect to the prospects for positive social change. While numerous cultural and political divisions certainly exist within and across societies in the region, there was enough in the way of shared grievances to unite large segments of the population in each country in a common quest for more genuinely representative and democratic systems of government. Under these circumstances, WikiLeaks' contributions in terms of exposing corruption and inspiring action were welcomed.

A very different political climate prevailed in America during roughly the same period. As noted by Fenster (2012) and Roberts (2011), WikiLeaks' largest revelations occurred in a period of economic uncertainty and physical insecurity in the US. Citizens appeared more concerned about the organization's potential to harm American national interests than they were with its ostensibly democratic role as an advocate of transparency and free speech. Commenting on the Cablegate leaks of November 2010, Roberts (2011, 20) argues that what the cables revealed, including US spying on United Nations diplomats, covert military action against alleged terrorists and negotiations with regimes guilty of human rights abuses, might not be regarded by much of the public as abuses at all but rather as proof that their government was "prepared to get its hands dirty to protect its citizens". By implication, this includes a readiness to tolerate repeated US attempts to coerce governments and act militarily if such actions can be construed as serving American interests. By contrast, US military interventions and support for dictators in the MENA region have long been a source of popular resentment there, a key factor contributing to Arab openness to WikiLeaks.

In keeping with the points raised above, polls such as those conducted by CNN, CBS and Pew Research in 2011 suggest that in general Americans dislike and/or distrust WikiLeaks. As Roberts (2011, 20) observes, the more WikiLeaks disclosed in 2010, the more public opinion hardened against it. By contrast, the organization's popularity in the Arab world during roughly the same timeframe was high. A survey conducted by the Doha Debates found that 60% of those polled believed that "the world is better off with WikiLeaks", with nearly 75% of respondents stating a desire to see WikiLeaks publish more on the Arab world (York 2013, 231). While the polling results cited here were inevitably influenced by a broad range of political, economic and social realities, the news media appears to have played a particularly important role in shaping attitudes in each context. This is most apparent when contrasting the active role adopted by AJ in terms of applauding and in some respects facilitating the Arab Spring uprisings, with the more conservative role of the US media in terms of naturalizing America's presumed right to project its military power globally while pursuing its alleged Global War on Terror by all available means.

As previously indicated, AJ was openly sympathetic to the protesters in Tunisia, Egypt and elsewhere during most of the Arab Spring, a fact which earned it the wrath of state leaders throughout the region. The station was also a pioneer in terms of integrating news gathering and reporting practices with the use of social media. In both respects, the organization remained closely attuned to the Arab street as events unfolded. As Castells (2012, 27) observes, a symbiotic relationship evolved between the protesters and the news station's staff of reporters. Citizens often took on the role of journalists, using mobile phones to upload images and information to AJ or YouTube. In turn, AJ went so far as to develop a programme allowing mobile phones to connect directly to its satellite (Castells 2012, 28). Moreover, whenever activists were abused by police, or citizens felt that their revolution was endangered by state activity, protesters would appear on AJ to express their fears and outrage before millions of Arab viewers (Dabashi 2012, 99).

It is important to emphasize that AJ's behaviour during the early Arab Spring was highly atypical for a news organization. Not because the network attempted to directly incite the masses as some Arab leaders claimed, but simply because most of the output from large, mainstream news organizations, whether commercial or state-owned, reflects the outlook of the dominant interests of the societies in which they operate. In the case of AJ, however, the incentives and pressures which normally guarantee this situation were largely absent. Structured similarly to public service media like the BBC, AJ is a non-commercial enterprise which also operates at arm's length from direct state control. This made it easier for the organization to champion the cause of major political change in the region while consolidating its credibility as a true voice of ordinary Arabs. Nonetheless, events suggest that AJ is not entirely immune to pressure from its host state, and by extension, from Qatar's wealthy neighbours. The station provided far less coverage of the brutally suppressed uprisings in the Gulf state of Bahrain than it did in the cases of Tunisia, Egypt, Libya or Syria (Lynch 2012).

It is in the latter respect, namely, studied inattention to the uprisings in Bahrain for the sake of political expediency, that AJ's behaviour was arguably more in keeping with patterns of reporting long associated with large-scale news operations. This point is critical. As media critics such as Herman and Chomsky (1988) and McChesney (2008) have repeatedly demonstrated, the propaganda aspect of news is rarely the result of direct lying or dishonesty on the part of reporters, but rather represents the outcome of direct and indirect economic and political pressures and news gathering routines which ensure that some topics receive more attention than others, and that those which do receive attention are framed in a manner which favours existing arrangements of power. A blatant example, and one which holds considerable relevance here, concerns the run-up to the US attack on Iraq in 2003. The public was then led to believe in the existence of a direct link, later revealed as fabricated, between the government of Saddam Hussein and the Al-Qaeda hijackers of 9/11. Citizens were also repeatedly subjected to the false claim that Iraq had amassed a hidden stockpile of weapons of mass destruction (WMDs).

To be clear, it was politicians such as George Bush and Dick Cheney, along with representatives of the US intelligence community, who misled the public. News organizations such as the *New York Times* did not lie; they merely repeated the statements of politicians faithfully, while giving them front page coverage. What the press did not do was subject official claims to vigorous scrutiny or appraisal. Thus, as numerous polls make clear, the American public internalized the propaganda claims in question and ultimately came to support their government's call for war (Marmura 2010a). What is left unreported is as critical in terms of making propaganda effective as is its positive content. For example, in the wake of the Arab Spring, Turkey, Israel and Saudi Arabia, all close US allies, provided Al-Qaeda-affiliated groups fighting the Syrian government with various forms of military, medical and logistical support. Yet, harsh statements against these ostensible "state sponsors of terror" were essentially absent from the American news media, particularly before the Obama administration shifted its military focus from overthrowing the Syrian government to fighting ISIS.

Many suggest that the value of *Collateral Murder* lies precisely in the fact that it was not a product of mainstream journalism. Rather, it represented a genuinely transgressive act which presented the realities of US military activity in a radically new light. There is certainly something in this claim. For example, in addition to the self-censorship and reflexive support for military engagements that has long characterized mainstream news reporting, the press pool system put in place during the first US conflict in Iraq in 1991 all but guaranteed that the public would be shielded from the "wrong images" (MacArthur 1992). In contrast to the relative freedom enjoyed by journalists during the Viet Nam war, reporters in conflict zones must now embed themselves within military units which serve as escorts. They travel only where the military deems it safe, and inevitably come to view the events in which they are immersed from the perspective of their soldier protectors. In addition, all news reports must undergo a security review, meaning that their content may be edited or censored. It is notable that by 2008, the *New York Times* had only managed to publish five images of war dead after the 2003 invasion, and that in four of those cases, the photographer was "kicked out of his or her embed" following their publication (Kamber and Arango 2008).

Such realities draw attention back to the possibility that by its very nature *Collateral Murder* opened a space for serious critical appraisal of relevant government policies within the public sphere. While this conclusion might at first appear warranted, it is important not to confuse the salient issues. On the one hand, there is no question that the video, like other WikiLeaks' disclosures, provided valuable ammunition for those already critical of their government's policies. In addition, the authenticity, novelty and poignancy of *Collateral Murder* arguably enhance its status, potentially enabling it to have at least some public impact over the longer term. The video remains available on YouTube and continues to receive attention within various online forums. It also received immediate and widespread attention from mainstream news outlets due to its graphic and controversial nature. However, none of these realities should be taken as evidence that *Collateral Murder* introduced serious critique of US foreign policy into mainstream discourse, at least during the timeframe in which it became a major news story. This is a key point, since it is the mainstream media which continues to play a dominant role in the formation of public opinion.

It was noted earlier that philosopher Slavoj Zizek (2013) lauds *Collateral Murder* as an important achievement. Commenting on the ways in which inconvenient truths may be downplayed or obscured through media-speak, he argues that the video made them impossible to ignore and to "pretend not to know what everyone knows we know" (2013, 256). This is an intriguing though problematic assertion. It rests on the premise that people tend to disavow or turn away from knowledge which makes them feel helpless, conflicts with dearly held beliefs, suggests their own complicity in a larger problem or otherwise makes them uncomfortable. This may include not only politicians and media workers engaged in propaganda campaigns, but also ordinary citizens. Hence, on the one hand, texts such as *Collateral Murder* offer a possible means for initiating dialogue and reflection on difficult topics. On the other hand, even as visceral and ostensibly unambiguous a text as *Collateral Murder* may be reinscribed within mythic habits of thought and narrative structures in the media that serve to support the status quo.

The idea that photographs, and by extension video recordings, somehow speak for themselves, offering irrefutable proof of a given reality, is a widely held conviction, one captured by the phrase "a picture is worth a thousand words". Yet, as Susan Sontag (1977) demonstrated in her seminal work on the subject, images and recordings are as open to interpretation and ideological contestation as are written accounts of events. To cite only one example, it is worth recalling the case of Rodney King, a black Los Angeles resident whose savage beating by police officers in the aftermath of a high-speed car chase was caught on film. The reaction from the local black community and from many other Americans was outrage. However, when four of the officers were tried on charges of police brutality, the mostly white jury who had viewed the video repeatedly in the courtroom did not find King to be a sympathetic figure. Rather, they identified with the efforts and predicament of the white police officers in their ongoing efforts to "control" King (Jacobs 2000). The eventual acquittal of the officers is generally regarded as the main trigger behind the Los Angeles riots of 1992, which resulted in the deaths of 53 people with over 2000 injured.

Mohamed Bouazizi's self-immolation did not need to be caught on film to spark the first Arab uprisings in Tunisia. Hearing about the incident or watching the resulting street protests on television was enough to strike a chord with citizens across the region, making Bouazizi's tragic death a potent symbol of their common frustrations. But whether one is dealing with images, radio broadcasts, Twitter hashtags, word of mouth or stories in print, ideology provides the filter. Sontag (1977) illustrates the importance of this reality when comparing the cases of the Korean and Viet Nam wars. Both involved the commitment of large numbers of American troops, and both resulted in the wide-scale devastation of a foreign society. Sontag acknowledges the important role played by photographs in terms of affecting public opinion about events in Viet Nam, and hence in speeding America's military withdrawal from that country. She also suggests, however, that the existence of similar photographs would likely have proven ineffectual in the case of Korea.

Sontag (1977) maintains that at the time of the Korean conflict, the "ideological space" necessary for pictures of war atrocities to inspire protest was absent. US involvement in Korea took place during the height of the cold war and was widely understood as an unambiguous part of the struggle between the Free World and Communist totalitarianism. Sontag (1977, 18) argues that in such an atmosphere, "photographs of the cruelty of unlimited American firepower would have been irrelevant". In the case of Viet Nam, even an image as wrenching as the well-known photograph of a young girl running naked and screaming towards the photographer's camera while burning from napalm required the appropriate political context to help fuel anti-war activism. That context was present. Various sources of discontent with the political status quo were bringing about rapid social change and conflict in the US. An emerging youth culture, anti-racist civil rights activism, a rejuvenated feminist movement, experimentation with new lifestyles and forms of spirituality, all overlapped with and laid the groundwork for a vibrant anti-war movement. The latter was anti-colonialist in outlook and distrustful of its government's motives in Asia.

In line with Sontag's reasoning, it is apparent that the political context needed for *Collateral Murder* to resonate strongly with the American public and inspire political action was lacking at the time of the video's release. This is not to suggest that US citizens are or were incapable of feeling sympathy for those depicted in the film. However, in the absence of any sustained or serious critique of US policies, the victims in question were likely to be regarded as the unfortunate but inevitable casualties of a war in which America's good intentions need not be questioned, even if Iraqis are too backward to reject extremism and accept democracy, and even if a few bad apples in the US military committed crimes against civilians. As McChesney (2008) observes, the US tends to be treated by its domestic press as an essentially philanthropic power with no military or economic designs. He points out that in the case of the 2003 invasion of Iraq almost no attention was given in the popular media to such basic considerations as "the imperial drive encouraged by a massive military-industrial complex; the geopolitical and economic advantages of having permanent military bases and a client/friendly ally in the heart of the Middle East; the domestic political advantages for a president to have the populace whipped into wartime fervor; the security needs of Israel, a close ally of the United States; and, of course, oil" (McChesney 2008, 115).

A genuinely adversarial press might have utilized frames of reference other than those advanced by state actors claiming to be engaged in a war on terror. For example, through the lens of international law, or by referring to America's long record of divide and rule policies in the region. Instead, the rhetorical playing field was left wide open to lines of argumentation and propaganda that might otherwise be dismissed as spurious. Ironically in this regard, a number of those defending the Apache helicopter pilots' actions protested that the video footage lacked appropriate context. According to former US Secretary of Defense Robert Gates, viewing the video means that "you're looking at a situation through a soda straw, and you have no context or perspective". A report from the *Washington Post* stated that "it was unclear whether the journalists had been killed by US fire or by shooting from the Iraqis targeted by the Apache" (Partlow and Finkel 2007). As noted earlier the video was also criticized by FOX News for its "selective editing" and failure to draw attention to those in the video who appeared to be armed (Fishel 2010).

From the standpoint of international law, such criticism is superfluous since the entire US invasion was illegal. The Bush administration ignored the United Nations Charter which prohibit launching a war unless in self-defence, or by authorization from the Security Council. UN Secretary General Kofi Annan stated of the invasion in September 2004 that, "from our point of view and the UN Charter point of view it was illegal". According to the UN Charter, violation of the prohibition against the use of force amounts to the crime of aggression. The definition put forward in the Nuremberg Trials affirms that aggression is "not only an international crime; it is the *supreme* international crime, differing only from other crimes in that it contains within itself the accumulated evil of the whole" (Rockler 1999). It is also worth observing that the case of the 2003 attack on Iraq was far from exceptional in terms of US conduct. While rarely commented upon in the mainstream news media, the US has a long record of violating international law when it deems it expedient, though it regularly invokes alleged violations by other nations as a pretext for military action or economic sanctions (Herman and Peterson 2010).

Even at the level of hard-headed pragmatism and realpolitik, defences of the military's actions such as those previously cited are essentially empty. They rest on the premise that US soldiers were in Iraq to eliminate Saddam Hussein's alleged cache of WMD and the related threat posed by terrorism. Attention to these two sets of concerns, which were frequently conflated—that is, terrorists might gain access to WMD—overwhelmingly dominated American media commentary during the lead-up to and early phase of the war (Moeller 2004). However, it was not until US forces had largely decimated Iraq and what remained of Saddam's police state apparatus that Al-Qaeda was able to gain a foothold in the country, in turn paving the way for the rise of its offshoot, ISIS. In other words, the US invasion brought Al-Qaeda to Iraq, increasing its strength and influence in the region, exactly reversing what was claimed. As I have emphasized elsewhere, the American public remains grossly ill-informed on such matters, with numerous polls indicating that belief in a Saddam/Al-Qaeda link continued to grow long after this propaganda claim had been discredited (Marmura 2010b).

The absence of a strong watchdog role on the part of the news media may have additional, more insidious consequences in terms of how a media event such as *Collateral Murder* may come to be understood at the popular level. Denuded of their more radical implications, such revelations may serve to reinforce myths and truisms concerning the presumed merits of the existing political system, rather than inspire a more critical mindset. Roland Barthes (1957) illustrates the underlying logic in a short essay entitled "Operation Astra", a piece which drew on the example of a French advertising campaign for Astra margarine. The problem facing those hoping to increase sales of their product was that margarine is "not butter" but rather something widely viewed as cheap and inferior. The genius of the advertisements lay in the fact that these shortcomings were openly confronted. Barthes notes that the ads would begin with an indignant outcry by a household member such as "A mousse made with margarine? Unthinkable! Your Uncle will be furious!" However, old prejudices are soon dispelled. Only our silly hang-ups prevented us from seeing the benefits of this economical, nourishing and versatile product. So what if it is basically just grease?

The rhetorical strategy at play in the advertisement is a common but effective one. Barthes (1957) suggests that it is most often invoked in defence of some institution or aspect of the status quo that is easily subjected to progressive criticism. In what essentially amounts to an "inoculation process", attention is first drawn to the flaws of whatever it is being defended or promoted. Then, with potential opponents disarmed, the source of contention is "rescued" by a sudden about-face in which its importance or usefulness is elevated above its shortcomings. Barthes cites media commentary on the military as a classic example. Its harsh discipline, brutal and primitive functions and anti-democratic character make it easy to criticize. Yet, after highlighting its major shortcomings, its virtues may be more clearly revealed. As the necessary sacrifice needed to protect democracy, the military represents the most patriotic institution imaginable. It is the entity that keeps our country strong and free, guarantees our leadership on the world stage, gives our young men and women a noble purpose, and so on.

An opinion piece in the commentary section of the *Wall Street Journal* dealing directly with the case of Collateral Murder reproduced the Astra formula perfectly.

Written by conservative author Gabriel Schoenfeld (2010), the piece is entitled "Warfare Through 'a Soda Straw'" in deference to the comments made by Robert Gates cited earlier. Having affirmed the importance of "maximum openness" in democratic societies, Schoenfeld warns that there are dangers when access to information is uninformed. Conceding that "the video of the Iraq firefight brings horrifically before our eyes the reality of war in ways that make us confront the basic questions of how and why we fight", he then advises that there is "another side to the coin". After reaffirming Gates' claim that those killed were likely perceived as armed by the Apache pilots, Schoenfeld insists that the video masks the greater virtues of the military, stating, "The WikiLeaks videos also do not reveal the hundreds upon hundreds of cases in which American forces refrain from attacking targets precisely because civilians are in harm's way." He then suggests that such concern for civilians is even costing US soldiers' lives in Afghanistan.

When reflecting on the points raised above, it is worth recalling Zizek's high regard for *Collateral Murder*. It is interesting that during the same interview in which he praises the video, when both he and Assange are interviewed together by Amy Goodman, Zizek (2013) also issues a warning to those wedded to conventional, liberal ideals of truth-telling. In doing so, he alludes to the same patterns of ideological thought identified by Barthes. Citing such popular thrillers as *The Pelican Brief* and *All the President's Men*, Zizek notes that these films might at first appear to be critical of the status quo since they portray even such powerful and celebrated personages as the President as deeply implicated in corruption. However, such films are very much in keeping with prevailing ideology and popular mythology. Posing the rhetorical question of why one exits the movie theatre in such high spirits, Zizek (2013, 258) refers to the larger underlying message of such films: "Look what a great country we are! An ordinary guy can topple the mightiest men in the world."

We often witness similar appeals to ideology when politicians are confronted with mass demonstrations against an unpopular policy or issue. Rather than address the matters at stake, much is made instead of how wonderful it is to live in a society where the people can assemble and express themselves so freely. It is unclear why Zizek refrains from warning about the application of this logic to case of *Collateral Murder*, especially since he discusses the traps posed by WikiLeaks' ostensibly piecemeal, "conspiratorial" approach to revealing wrongdoing elsewhere (Zizek 2011). Perhaps it is out of deference to his co-interviewee, or perhaps it is because he overlooks the relevance of his own arguments. Yet, as noted above, the absence of serious news critique invited precisely this type of response. The public is encouraged to celebrate the inherent goodness of a society in which major scandals can be aired before all to be debated, although within decisively narrow parameters as suggested earlier, and discussed openly. Certainly, it is a reading of democracy far less threatening than the stark alternative of attempting to hold power accountable for its excesses. As Barthes (1957, 53) puts it, "What does it matter *after all*, that an Order is somewhat brutal, somewhat blind, if it allows us to live inexpensively?"

When the public responds with outrage to an event, or when widespread attitudes towards a given set of issues appear to be changing, there is clearly more at work than the way such issues are portrayed in the mainstream media. As demonstrated throughout this chapter, a myriad of factors is inevitably at play, including longer-term economic, political and cultural trends which necessarily condition public responses to stories in the news including potential sources of moral shock. Nonetheless, the news media is clearly a critical if not a central factor in shaping public reactions to events. In addition to making us aware of more immediate stories and scandals, the media also condition attitudes over time, providing the public with the necessary narrative structures and points of reference needed to make sense of any given issue. In the process, they help establish an ideological climate either conducive or hostile to political change. The next chapter considers the importance of this reality with respect to WikiLeaks' direct involvement with the mainstream media, with attention devoted to news framing practices surrounding Cablegate during its first month of coverage by the *New York Times*.

References

Assange, Julian. 2010. Collateral Murder? In-depth Analysis of a Leaked Military Video Showing a US Army Helicopter Firing on Iraqis. *Al Jazeera English*, April 19. http://www.aljazeera.com/programmes/general/2010/04/20104159123873370.html.

Barthes, Roland. 1957. *Mythologies*. New York: Hill and Wang.

Benkler, Yochai. 2013. WikiLeaks and the Networked Fourth Estate. In *Beyond WikiLeaks: Implications of Communications, Journalism and Society*, ed.

Benedetta Brevini, Arne Hintz, and Patrick McCurdy, 11–34. New York: Palgrave Macmillan.

Castells, Manuel. 2012. *Networks of Outrage and Hope*. Cambridge: Polity Press.

Christensen, Christian. 2014. WikiLeaks and the Afterlife of Collateral Murder. *International Journal of Communication* 8: 2593–2602. http://ijoc.org/index.php/ijoc/article/viewFile/3209/1243.

Dabashi, Hamid. 2012. *The Arab Spring: The End of Postcolonialism*. New York: Zed Books.

Dean, Jodi. 2002. *Publicity's Secret: How Technoculture Capitalizes on Democracy*. Ithaca/London: Cornell University Press.

———. 2009. *Democracy and Other Neoliberal Fantasies: Communicative Capitalism and Left Politics*. Durham/London: Duke University Press.

Dunn, Hopeton S. 2013. "Something Old, Something New…": WikiLeaks and the Collaborating Newspapers – Exploring the Limits of Conjoint Approaches to Political Exposure. In *Beyond WikiLeaks: Implications of Communications, Journalism and Society*, ed. Benedetta Brevini, Arne Hintz, and Patrick McCurdy, 85–100. New York: Palgrave Macmillan.

El-Nawawy, Mohammed, and Adel Iskander. 2003. *Al-Jazeera: The Story of the Network that Is Rattling Governments and Redefining Modern Journalism*. Boulder: Westview Press.

Fenster, Mark. 2012. Disclosure's Effects: WikiLeaks and Transparency. *Iowa Law Review* 97: 753–807. https://ssrn.com/abstract=1797945.

Fishel, Justin. 2010. Military Raises Questions About Credibility of Leaked Iraq Shooting Video. *Fox News*, April 7. http://www.foxnews.com/politics/2010/04/07/military-raises-questions-credibility-leaked-iraq-shooting-video.html.

Herman, Edward S., and Noam Chomsky. 1988. *Manufacturing Consent: The Political Economy of the Mass Media*. New York: Pantheon Books.

Herman, Edward S., and David Peterson. 2010. *The Politics of Genocide*. New York: Monthly Review Press.

Howard, Philip N., and Muzammil M. Hussain. 2011. The Upheavals in Egypt and Tunisia: The Role of Digital Media. *Journal of Democracy* 22 (3) https://muse.jhu.edu/article/444758.

———. 2013. *Democracy's Fourth Wave?* Oxford: Oxford University Press.

Jacobs, Ronald N. 2000. *Race, Media and the Crisis of Civil Society*. Cambridge: Cambridge University Press.

Kamber, Michael, and Tim Arango. 2008. 4,000 U.S. Deaths, and a Handful of Images. *New York Times*, July 26. http://www.nytimes.com/2008/07/26/world/middleeast/26censor.html.

Keller, Bill. 2011. Dealing with Assange and the Wikileaks Secrets. *The New York Times*, January 26. http://www.nytimes.com/2011/01/30/magazine/30Wikileaks-t.html?pagewanted=all.

Lee, Francis L. F. 2014. Triggering the Protest Paradigm: Examining Factors Affecting News Coverage of Protests. *International Journal of Communication* 8: 2725–2756. http://ijoc.org/index.php/ijoc/article/view/2873/1215.

Lynch, Marc. 2006. *Voices of the New Arab Public*. New York: Columbia University Press.

———. 2012. Political Science and the New Arab Public Sphere. *Publicsphere.ssrc. org*, 12 June. http://publicsphere.ssrc.org/lynch-political-science-and-the-new-arab-public-sphere/.

Lynch, Lisa. 2013. The Leak Heard Round the World? Cablegate in the Evolving Global Mediascape. In *Beyond WikiLeaks: Implications of Communications, Journalism and Society*, ed. Benedetta Brevini, Arne Hintz, and Patrick McCurdy, 56–77. New York: Palgrave Macmillan.

MacArthur, John R. 1992. *Second Front: Censorship, and Propaganda in the Gulf War*. New York: Hill and Wang.

Marmura, Stephen. 2010a. Tales of 9/11 – What Conspiracy Theories in Egypt and the United States Tell Us About 'Media Effects'. *Arab Media & Society*, August. https://www.arabmediasociety.com/tales-of-911-what-conspiracy-theories-in-egypt-and-the-united-states-tell-us-about-media-effects/.

———. 2010b. Security Vs Privacy: Media Messages, State Policies, and American Public Trust in Government. In *Surveillance, Privacy and the Globalization of Personal Information*, ed. Elia Zureik, Lynda Harling Stalker, Emily Smith, David Lyon, and Yolande Chan, 100–126. Montreal/Kingston: McGill-Queen's University Press.

McChesney, Robert W. 2008. *The Political Economy of Media: Enduring Issues, Emerging Dilemmas*. New York: Monthly Review Press.

Moeller, Susan. D. 2004. *Media Coverage of Weapons of Mass Destruction. A Report for the Center for International and Strategic Studies at Maryland*. http://www.pipa.org/articles/WMDstudy_full.pdf.

Partlow, Joshua, and David Finkel. 2007. U.S., Shiite Fighters Clash in Baghdad. *Washington Post*, July 13.

Roberts, Alasdair. 2011. The WikiLeaks Illusion. *The Wilson Quarterly* (Summer).

Rockler, Walter J. 1999. War Crime Law Applies to US Too. *Counterpunch*, June 15.

Saleh, Ibrahim. 2013. WikiLeaks and the Arab Spring: The Twists and Turns of Media, Culture and Power. In *Beyond WikiLeaks: Implications of Communications, Journalism and Society*, ed. Benedetta Brevini, Arne Hintz, and Patrick McCurdy, 236–244. New York: Palgrave Macmillan.

Shoenfeld, Gabriel. 2010. WikiLeaks Through 'a Soda Straw'. *The Wall Street Journal*, June 23. https://www.wsj.com/articles/SB10001424052748704895204575321080522272718.

Sontag, Susan. 1977. *On Photography*. New York: Farrar, Straus and Giroux.

Wing, Nick. 2013. Here's the Video of U.S. Troops Killing Innocent Iraqis. If Not for Bradley Manning, We Never Would Have Seen It. *The Huffington Post*,

August 21. http://www.huffingtonpost.ca/entry/bradley-manning-collateral
    murder_n_3790649.
York, Jillian C. 2013. The Internet and Transparency Beyond WikiLeaks. In
    Beyond WikiLeaks: Implications of Communications, Journalism and Society, ed.
    Benedetta Brevini, Arne Hintz, and Patrick McCurdy, 229–235. New York:
    Palgrave Macmillan.
Zizek, Slavoj. 2011. Good Manners in the Age of WikiLeaks. *London Review of
    Books* 33 (2): 9–10. https://www.lrb.co.uk/v33/n02/slavoj-zizek/good-
    manners-in-the-age-of-wikileaks.
———. 2013. Amy Goodman in Conversation with Julian Assange and Slavoj
    Zizek. In *Beyond WikiLeaks: Implications of Communications, Journalism and
    Society*, ed. Benedetta Brevini, Arne Hintz, and Patrick McCurdy, 254–271.
    New York: Palgrave Macmillan.

CHAPTER 4

The Non-revelations of Cablegate

Abstract WikiLeaks cooperated with the *New York Times* in 2010, providing the newspaper with access to 250,000 leaked US diplomatic cables. Content analysis of news coverage during the first month of reporting is presented. It is demonstrated that while "Cablegate" potentially opened the door for serious critique of US foreign policy, this possibility was never realized. Rather, established wisdom concerning the necessity of strong US world leadership is reinforced. The case of editorial content and news framing practices concerning Iran's nuclear capabilities stands out. The latter was commensurate with an ongoing, state-driven propaganda campaign. However, WikiLeaks did establish its reputation as the leading source for authentic leaked information, a reality holding long-term importance for the group.

Keywords Cablegate • *New York Times* • News frames • Foreign policy • Non-revelatory • Propaganda

The media event known as "Cablegate" commenced on November 28, 2010. This was the date when the *New York Times* along with *the Guardian*, *Der Spiegel*, *La Monde* and *El Pais*, began to report to their respective publics about leaked material drawn from a cache of over 250,000 classified US embassy cables. Cablegate was preceded by publication in the *Times* earlier that year of the Afghan War Logs and Iraq War Logs, and was drawn from the same cache of material provided to WikiLeaks by Private Bradley Manning in early 2010. However, unlike the previous two disclosures, which involved classified military reports, the embassy cables represented "the daily traffic between the State Department and more than 270 American diplomatic outposts around the world" (*New York Times* 2010). As such, Cablegate represented a particularly vexing source of embarrassment for US politicians and diplomats, exposing an apparent inability to communicate sensitive information and provide unofficial assessments of developing political situations in a discrete manner.

More than any previous leak, Cablegate incurred the wrath of the American state. Vice President Joe Biden referred to Julian Assange as a "high-tech terrorist", Hillary Clinton stated that WikiLeaks' actions were "an attack on the international community", and Speaker of the House Newt Gingrich declared that Assange should be treated as a foreign combatant. The incident cemented the determination of the Obama administration, itself responsible for prosecuting more whistle-blowers than all previous US administrations combined, to have Assange extradited to the US to face charges under the Espionage Act of 1917. In addition, an array of commercial interests, including PayPal, Amazon, MasterCard, Visa and the Bank of America, assisted the government in its attempts to terminate WikiLeaks' activities. One result was that the group's access to the domain names and server space it requires to store data was severely restricted, as was its ability to collect the public donations needed to pay its core staff (Fuchs 2014; Brevini and Murdoch 2013). Regardless of WikiLeaks' actual ability to harm US interests, it had come to be viewed as a genuine threat by those in power.

Given the seriousness of the official response to the leak, it is worth considering whether publication of the Cablegate material in a major American newspaper was ever likely to significantly raise public awareness or provoke widespread criticism of relevant state practices or policies. The question gains salience when considering ongoing changes to the media environment holding the potential to affect the character of news. A proliferation of alternative, citizen-produced information sources now presents major news operations with both bottom-up competition for audiences and fresh potential resources for journalists. In theory, this could lead to a broader range of viewpoints being expressed by mainstream news outlets. The growth of alternative information sites may also affect public opinion in other ways, most notably by exacerbating the trend of growing audience fragmentation. Nonetheless, major operations like the *New York Times* or CNN continue to enjoy the lion's share of audience viewership, and their large size and profit orientation ensure that they remain embedded in the same web of political and economic relationships as other large-scale commercial institutions. These realities were not altered by the arrival of the Internet and continue to shape processes of news selection and framing in virtually all media (Pedro 2011).

As discussed in Chap. 2, a key reason that Assange felt compelled to forge "partnerships" with major news organizations was his growing conviction that grassroots actors sympathetic to WikiLeaks were not up to the task of either interpreting leaked material knowledgably or communicating their analyses effectively to a mass public or publics. This situation, along with WikiLeaks' strategies in relation to it, has changed substantially over time, a matter to be taken up in Chap. 5. For now, it is enough to recall that in 2010 Assange seemed prepared to place a degree of faith in the mainstream news media that many WikiLeaks supporters felt was unwarranted. It is not enough, however, to affirm that WikiLeaks simply sold out in this regard, or to reject the possibility that Assange's gambit might have paid off. The mainstream press does at times offer real criticism of government and/or state polices, even if of a limited nature, and the very act of leaking classified material to leading newspapers might itself draw the public's attention to important matters of which citizens would otherwise remain unaware.

In this chapter, I demonstrate that while access to the Cablegate material potentially opened the door for serious media critique of various aspects of US policy, this possibility was never realized. Instead, reporting in the *New York Times* proved non-revelatory in a dual sense. First, because the idea that the leaked cables "told us nothing new" was a dominant theme in the coverage, particularly in the editorializing, even while the cable leak was presented as a major scoop. Second, and more importantly, because this editorial stance was self-fulfilling. Rather than using the contents of specific leaked documents as points of departure for interrogating what many might consider to be deeply disturbing aspects of US foreign policy, the resulting coverage served primarily to reinforce established wisdom concerning America's role as a benign world leader.

Rather than serving in any meaningful watchdog capacity, much of the coverage fed directly into an ongoing propaganda campaign against Iran.

Before proceeding further, it is necessary to comment on the nature of the news sample under consideration along with the approach to news content adopted here. In keeping with this book's primary focus on the

US context, attention in this chapter is restricted to reporting in the *New York Times*. The sample examined consists of news reports, editorials, analyses and a handful of featured letters to the editor, made available within an archive provided on *nytimes.com* under the heading "State's Secrets", and subheaded "A cache of diplomatic cables provides a chronicle of the United States' relations with the world". It includes all material pertaining to Cablegate between November 28, 2010, and January 3, 2011. All news pieces in the archive making direct reference to WikiLeaks, 276 in total, were reviewed and then sorted according to the subject matter they addressed. While some reports dealt with more than one of the topic areas identified in the next section, a consistent effort was made to categorize news items in terms of their primary focus.

There were distinct advantages to directly reviewing all relevant articles in State's Secrets. First, as stated above, it enabled categorization of the news items according to the main topic dealt with in each. This is something computerized word and subject searches often do poorly. Moreover, the main intent here is to convey a good general sense of the range and character of the overall reporting, rather than quantifying the use of key words or phrases. Relatedly, engaging in a close reading of all relevant articles made it possible to identify the basic assumptions and related interpretive frameworks that guided news reporting and editorializing on any given aspect of the leak. By extension, it allowed for careful consideration of the parameters within which relevant topics were discussed and debated. These issues receive attention in Part I of the analysis.

While other aspects of the leak did or might have received extensive news coverage, it is arguably what the leak did or did not reveal regarding the goals and nature of its government's own policies that could potentially vindicate WikiLeaks' claim to be reviving journalism's watchdog role of holding power more accountable. For this reason, coverage of leaks dealing specifically with foreign policy concerns is emphasized, providing the focus in Part II of the analysis. Here, attention is directed mainly to reporting on leaks concerning Iran's alleged nuclear weapons programme. This was State's Secrets leading story, at least with respect to cable content. However, as suggested above, the nature and significance of reporting on this topic cannot be fully appreciated in isolation from other aspects of the overall news sample. Hence, the observations and arguments put forward in this section proceed from those made in Part I.

The forthcoming analysis works from premises consistent with the findings of extensive critical political economy research on news production, and engages in a compatible "thematic" approach to news content (Philo 2007). Issues pertaining to the political economy of news are discussed at some length in earlier chapters. For present purposes, it is enough to emphasize several key points. One is that the ideological and discursive character of news cannot be properly assessed solely by attending to patterns of language use discernible within any given news sample. As Philo (2007) points out, analyses that remain entirely text-focused are limited in two important respects. First, they cannot establish the accuracy of a given news claim through appeals to relevant sources beyond the sample. Second, they fail to draw clear linkages between the preferred readings of events put forward in news accounts and the outlook and agendas of powerful institutions with which the interests of news corporations may be closely aligned.

The content of mainstream reporting does not simply reflect the cultural outlook of the societies within which news organizations operate. While popular sentiments and common-sense understandings of reality are drawn upon and appealed to by journalists, news messages also shape perceptions by selecting the topics that most occupy the public's attention. And by adhering to a defined narrative pattern, storyline or angle, news reports provide cues for how to think about these topics. Hence, what McCombs and Shaw (1972) term "agenda-setting" is directly linked to practices of news framing. Agenda-setting pertains to the salience of issues while framing is concerned with the presentation of issues (de Vreese 2005, 53). News frames organize otherwise fragmentary pieces of information together in a thematic way. Hence, a frame may be understood as "a central organizing idea or storyline that provides meaning to an unfolding strip of events, weaving a connection among them" (Gamson and Modligliani 1989). As such, news framing involves selecting certain aspects of an issue to hold people's attention while providing a guiding line of interpretation (Entman 1993).

Efforts to guide news viewers' or readers' understandings of events are most visible in the case of editorials and opinion pieces, where explicit attempts to interpret relevant information are undertaken on the public's behalf. However, it is also important to consider themes and narrative structures latent within routine reporting. Accounts of seemingly unrelated or only indirectly related sets of issues often comport with one another in terms of what they implicitly take for granted. It is the invisible or given nature of the assumptions informing news discourse that often serves to keep discussion and debate within decidedly narrow parameters.

These assumptions reinforce and naturalize a dominant worldview (Herman and Chomsky 1988). As Philo (2007, 181) notes with respect to research compiled by the Glasgow Media Group, the press may at times provide attention to disparate points of view and display balance regarding some issues, ostensibly satisfying the journalistic ethic of fairness. However, on sensitive issues of state, or where powerful groups are in strong agreement, news accounts tend to be more one-dimensional. The importance of these points with respect to Cablegate will become apparent as the discussion proceeds.

PART I: REPORTING IN "STATE'S SECRETS": TOPICS, THEMES AND DEBATES

One hundred days after their appearance in the American and European press, only 2% of the 250,000 leaked diplomatic cables had been published by participating newspapers (Lynch 2013). Even for large operations like *The Guardian* or the *New York Times*, providing rapid, accessible coverage on all leaked material was a practical impossibility, a reality that underscores the importance of selection and framing in the creation of news. It is therefore noteworthy that of the 276 news pieces located in the State's Secrets archive, less than half (132) focus on the content of the leaked cables. The other 144 pieces address developments and controversies pertaining to other aspects of the leaks' purported significance and impact. News pieces falling into the latter category will be considered in this section. Emphasis will be given to the ways that relevant reporting and editorializing served to reinforce the impression that the *Times* was fulfilling its watchdog role, even as it served to limit and shape, both directly and indirectly, coverage of issues explicitly related to cable content.

The topics covered in the 144 news articles referred to above break down approximately, with some overlap, as follows. Fifty-seven articles address legal and practical aspects of the government's attempts to shut down WikiLeaks, including the possibility that Assange could be extradited to the US to stand trial on espionage charges. Prominent among these are reports on measures taken against WikiLeaks by Visa, Paypal, Bank of America, and so on, and the countermeasures taken in WikiLeaks' defence by the hacktivist group Anonymous. Fifty-four pieces focus on the implications of the leaks for US diplomacy and/or government transparency, or the implications for other real or potential targets of WikiLeaks' disclosures. Included in this category are articles referring to the reactions of foreign governments to the leak. Another 18 articles address freedom of speech issues, specifically focusing on the implications of WikiLeaks' activities for the future of journalism. The 15 remaining items consist primarily of short, light-hearted references to WikiLeaks or its leader, including jokes, songs, movies and books invoking the organization, speculations concerning Assange's whereabouts and musings about Assange as a subject of news photography (Table 4.1).

The line separating news pieces dealing with cable content and those addressing other aspects of the leak in State's Secrets is sometimes blurry. For example, as indicated above, documents dealing with the reactions of foreign governments to Cablegate were placed in the same category as those dealing with other aspects of the leak's implications or "impacts". However, the reactions in question often pertained to specific cable content. These news pieces were classified as they were because their content focused less on the political significance of relevant statements or related policies themselves than on the potential embarrassment or negative diplomatic fallout that their disclosure might have caused. Articles in this category tended to play up the human-conflict aspect of reactions to leaked material while engaging in speculation as to whether the leak would have more than a temporary or superficial impact on US diplomacy.

There are several reasons to expect that a large portion of the reporting would focus on matters other than the cable content per se. First, much of the "diplomacy" in question was likely mundane, involving little more than communications on routine matters. By contrast, contemporary journalism tends to emphasize the dramatic, novel, entertaining and human-interest related aspects of issues and events as a means of encouraging and retaining the interest of readers or viewers (Curran 2005). This

Table 4.1 Articles in state's secrets

Total articles reviewed	276	
Articles focusing on content of leaked cables	132	
Articles referring to Iran		49
Articles referring to other countries		83
Articles focusing on other aspects of leak	144	
Legal/practical and dramatic aspects of attempts to shut down WikiLeaks		57
Implications for US diplomacy and/or other WikiLeaks targets		54
Freedom of speech and challenges to journalism		18
Human interest and popular culture		15

was clear in the case of reporting on the tit for tat "cyber-warfare" engaged in between organizations like Paypal and Visa on the one hand and Anonymous on the other. Similarly, as Beckett and Ball (2012, 85–86) point out, after Dec. 7, 2010, when Assange was arrested in England due to allegations of sexual misconduct made against him in Sweden, debates about WikiLeaks in the media became far more personal. While news coverage of WikiLeaks itself is not the main concern of this chapter, this observation is consistent with the extensive attention given to Assange's legal problems, character and personality quirks in State's Secrets.

It must also be acknowledged that many of the topic areas identified above did deserve substantial coverage when considered in terms of the public interest. Numerous articles address such matters as the strength or weakness of the state's case against WikiLeaks, and related ethical and legal concerns surrounding freedom of speech. And defences of press freedom were often vigorous. A guest editorial entitled *A Clear Danger to Free Speech* (Stone 2011) strongly criticized the "Shield Bill" then being introduced in Congress in response to Cablegate. As the article's author, Prof. of Law, Geoffrey R. Stone, points out, the bill would have amended the Espionage Act of 1917 to make it a crime for any person to knowingly and wilfully to disseminate, "in any manner prejudicial to the safety or interest of the United States", any classified information concerning the human intelligence activities of the US. Stone (2011) argues that the bill would violate the First Amendment by allowing for the punishment of "anyone who might publish or otherwise circulate the information after it had been leaked".

Such matters clearly hold importance for the future of journalism and hence for the ability of operations like the *New York Times* to conduct their business responsibly and without undue restrictions imposed by state authorities citing national security. However, it also bears emphasis that such defences of free speech, while arguably beneficial to the public, also reflect self-interest on the part of news organizations. They typically amount to a defence of, rather than a challenge to, the existing legal status quo. Moreover, the *Times* managed to defend its right and duty to publish the cable material even as it distanced itself from the goals and methods of Assange and his organization. This may be seen in the following statements by executive editor Bill Keller:

> WikiLeaks is not a "media partner" of The Times. We signed no agreement of any kind, with WikiLeaks or anyone else. In fact, in this case—our third round of articles based on documents obtained by WikiLeaks—we did not

receive the documents from WikiLeaks. Julian Assange, the founder of the group, decided to withhold the material from us, apparently because he was offended by our reporting on his legal and organizational problems. The London newspaper, The Guardian, gave us a copy of the archive, because they considered it a continuation of our collaboration on earlier WikiLeaks disclosures. (Keller 2010)

Other *Times* staff showed less restraint in their criticism of WikiLeaks, for example, in the text of a conversational exchange between editors David Brooks and Gail Collins entitled "Have We Learned Anything from the Leaked Cables?". Here, Brooks opines:

I don't think we should have access to the cables. I fervently believe that and find myself repulsed by the folks at WikiLeaks. They are bad for the world because they destroy trust, which isn't in great supply to start with, and I wish the establishment still had enough self-confidence to marginalize this sort of behavior and protect the social ecology. (Brooks and Collins 2010)

Similarly, in a piece entitled "American Diplomacy Revealed – as Good", editor Roger Cohen remarks:

Julian Assange, the thin-skinned founder of WikiLeaks, has hurt US interests across a broad but probably shallow spectrum. That will satisfy him in that he's a self-styled foe of the United States. The guy makes me queasy. (Cohen 2010)

While the editorial staff often took pains to distinguish their ostensibly responsible approach to leaked information from that of WikiLeaks, there were numerous defences of WikiLeaks in State's Secrets—typically from guest columnists or in the form of featured letters to the editor—and an effort was made in the paper to present "both sides" of the issue. However, as with other aspects of the coverage, attention to WikiLeaks' activities and motives adhere to conventional patterns of news discourse that are unlikely to encourage much in the way of critical reflection on the nature of US policy and diplomacy. An article written by *Times* staff editor Tobin Harshaw entitled "The Hunt for Julian Assange" is instructive in this regard. The piece appears in the *Times* "Opinionator" section, under the subheading "The Thread". Here, Harshaw explains that "the Thread is an in-depth look at how major news and controversies are being debated across the online spectrum". The introduction is worth presenting in its entirety:

One big lesson from the WikiLeaks dump of state department documents: Weddings in Dagestan are insanely awesome.

Most commentators, however, have grappled with weightier issues: Is it good or bad for the future of American diplomacy; will it lead to more sunshine in foreign policy or less? Do the cables represent a huge embarrassment for their authors or do our diplomats come off as shrewd, sensible professionals? Were the news organizations (including the one that supports the lifestyle I've become accustomed to) that printed the cables guilty of abetting a crime or were they serving a public interest? Should the world be heartened or horrified that Arab countries apparently take a much tougher line with Iran than they have publicly admitted? Is the idea that American diplomats were asked to spy on their United Nations colleagues an outrage or simple common sense? Was Joe Lieberman right or wrong to pressure Amazon.com to stop hosting WikiLeaks on its servers? Is Julian Assange, WikiLeaks's editor, a hero standing up to a broken and evil establishment or a sort of digital terrorist with "blood on his hands"? (Harshaw 2010)

I draw attention to this piece here for two reasons. First, because the author provides a sample survey and commentary regarding the general character of American media coverage of the leak, and the debates he refers to strongly reflect those appearing in State's Secrets. Second, because debates such as those described above are inherently unlikely to lead to any real critique of the political system, or to any serious questioning of state policies that transcend partisan disputes. While this situation might seem unremarkable, it clearly represents a problem for WikiLeaks, an organization dedicated to radicalizing or at least altering the mindset of the public. As Assange states in an interview with TIME in 2010, "It is not our goal to achieve a more transparent society; it's our goal to achieve a more just society. And most of the times, transparency and openness tends to lead in that direction, because abusive plans or behaviour get opposed" (Beckett and Ball 2012, 146). This goal is unlikely to be advanced when leaked material, or more accurately commentary regarding its import, is simply absorbed into narrow disputes about what is best for the US wherein both the rightness of the political system and the nature of American interests are already taken for granted.

There are no fresh insights concerning the nature of the state decision-making processes or of the forces and interests driving US policies. Debates about whether the leaks will ultimately prove good or bad for US diplomacy, whether US diplomats should feel embarrassed or proud of the cable disclosures, and so on, are better geared to reinforcing standard tropes about American exceptionalism and the valuable leadership role played by the US in global affairs. A prime example appears in an opinion piece entitled "We've Only Got America A" by *Times* editor, Thomas Friedman. After describing a world in which "superempowered" individuals like Assange exert disproportionate influence, and wherein emerging powers like China do not share America's tolerance of dissent, Friedman reasons as follows:

> But here's the fact: A China that can choke off conversations far beyond its borders, and superempowered individuals who can expose conversations far beyond their borders—or create posses of "cyber-hacktivists" who can melt down the computers of people they don't like—are now a reality. They are rising powers. A stable world requires that we learn how to get the best from both and limit the worst; it will require smart legal and technological responses.
>
> For that job, there is no alternative to a strong America. Critics said of the British Labour Party of the 1960s that the Britain they were trying to build was half-Sweden and half-heaven. The alternative today to a world ordered by American power is not some cuddly multipolar system—half-Sweden and half-heaven. It is half-China and half-superempowered individuals. (Friedman 2010)

The important point here is not whether Friedman's position is strong or weak. Nor is it a question of whether this or other pieces in State's Secrets represent good journalism in terms of the quality of the news writing or analyses provided. Rather, what is at issue is the range of opinion available to the reader and what proportion of news coverage, if any, is likely to draw attention to what are arguably destructive or negative aspects of US state decision-making practices or policy implementation. The record in this regard is instructive. As McChesney (2008, 101–107) observes, the arrival of professional journalism coincided with the emergence of the US as a global military power, and it is unusual today for journalists to provide perspectives on foreign policy matters that have not first been articulated within official Washington debate. It is worth pointing out that of the debates listed above by Harshaw (2010), only one, that concerning Arab attitudes towards Iran, pertains directly to cable content on policy matters. As will be argued in the next section, reporting on this issue fits seamlessly within a larger disinformation campaign concerning Iran's alleged nuclear weapons ambitions.

As illustrated with respect to *Collateral Murder*, drawing attention to ostensibly small imperfections or flaws in the system may be deployed rhetorically to underscore the good of the whole. This was clearly evident in the case of editorializing in State's Secrets. Many articles did refer to embarrassments caused by the cables and sometimes to larger crises of diplomacy. There was also ongoing debate as to how detrimental the leaks would ultimately prove for US foreign relations. Significantly, however, there was a strong consensus concerning what the leaks did or did not reveal to the public. Somewhat ironically, the dominant theme in this regard was that the leaked cables communicated little if anything new or important, at least in terms of the basic character of US relations with the rest of the world. Instead, the cable content is repeatedly depicted as banal or predictable even while cited as evidence of the inherent wisdom of American foreign policy and the skills and professionalism of US diplomats. For example, a piece by the editorial board entitled "WikiLeaks and the Diplomats" begins as follows:

> The business of diplomacy is often messy and when private communications become public, it can also be highly embarrassing.
> But what struck us, and reassured us, about the latest trove of classified documents released by WikiLeaks was the absence of any real skullduggery. After years of revelations about the Bush administration's abuses—including the use of torture and kidnappings—much of the Obama administration's diplomatic wheeling and dealing is appropriate and, at times, downright skillful. (Editorial Board 2010a)

Such framing is equally explicit in the previously cited piece entitled "Have We Learned Anything from the Leaked Cables?", involving an exchange between editors David Brooks and Gail Collins. The tail end of this conversation is provided below.

David Brooks: Maybe the good news is that there is no news. I've asked a few world leaders if the secret information they have access to gives them a different picture of the world than the one the rest of us get just reading the paper. They generally say no. What we see on the outside is what they see on the inside. They just have more granularity.

Gail Collins:	Yes, so far I've been amazed by how few surprises we've gotten. Unless you were under the impression that the other Arab countries didn't hate Iran. Or that China wasn't fully aware that the leadership of North Korea is entirely composed of nutballs.
David Brooks:	These cables—which don't include "top secret" stuff, admittedly —show no hidden conspiracies, at least of any consequence. Maybe the normal work of journalism covers the world as it really is.
Gail Collins:	And that's a thought that will make the folks at WikiLeaks very depressed. (Brooks and Collins 2010)

Similar comments recur throughout the editorial and opinion pieces in State's Secrets, including in a guest contribution by Albert R. Hunt entitled "Good Gossip, No Harm Done to US". After commenting on the temporary embarrassments that the leak has inevitably brought about, the author follows essentially the same script as Brooks and Collins, defending US conduct while taking a poke at WikiLeaks:

> Still, rather than exposing ineptitude, a reading of a fair portion of the documents suggests that they actually reflect well on US policy and diplomacy. Pressure to prevent Iran from obtaining nuclear weapons isn't effective if China, which gets much of its oil from that country, is opposed. US efforts to cut a deal with the Saudis, who fear Iran, to possibly supply more oil to China come across as shrewd.
>
> Most of the cables, along with the good gossip, reflect similar professionalism, probably to the consternation of the WikiLeaks crowd. (Hunt 2010)

Interestingly, the tendency to depict the cable content as representing little more than business as usual is in tension with the perceived need to present Cablegate as a major scoop. As suggested earlier, this tension was partially resolved by highlighting the importance of legal and free speech issues derived from the leak, and by devoting ongoing coverage to the related drama surrounding WikiLeaks' conflicts with various governments, individuals, businesses, and so on. However, it is also clear that at least some importance needed to be attributed to the cable content itself. The dominant rationale guiding commentary in this regard is that by making the material available to the public, along with sober analyses regarding its import, the *Times* provides its readers with the opportunity to gain a greater appreciation for the complexities and nuances of American foreign policy and the types of dilemmas facing US diplomats. This was the stance adopted in an opening piece entitled "A Note to Readers: The Decision to Publish Diplomatic Documents":

> The Times believes that the documents serve an important public interest, illuminating the goals, successes, compromises and frustrations of American diplomacy in a way that other accounts cannot match.
>   ... Of course, most of these documents will be made public regardless of what The Times decides. WikiLeaks has shared the entire archive of secret cables with at least four European publications, has promised country-specific documents to many other news outlets, and has said it plans to ultimately post its trove online. For The Times to ignore this material would be to deny its own readers the careful reporting and thoughtful analysis they expect when this kind of information becomes public. (Editorial Board 2010b)

Similar comments appear on the second day of reporting on the leak, in a question and answer exchange entitled "Answers to Readers Questions About State's Secrets". In response to a query about the possibility of losing cooperation with foreign governments, and citing the case of negative comments made by US officials about President Hamid Karsai in Afghanistan, Bill Keller makes the case that the public is "entitled to know the nature of our allies, even if that complicates the work of diplomats". He then states:

> While it is enlightening to see these observations in official cables, for the most part they enlarge rather than upend our understanding of complex foreign relations. For example, The Times has reported on numerous occasions that Iran's Arab neighbors share America's (and Israel's) worry about the prospect of a nuclear-armed Iran. The cables dramatize the depth of their concern, but the fact of their concern is not revelatory. (Keller 2010)

Such commentary is important since it reconciles the notion that the leaks held few surprises in terms of the types of problems or dilemmas they exposed, with the idea that they still held value when properly interpreted and presented to the public by a responsible news organization. By extension, the editorializing also serves to establish the framework within which (selected) leaks concerning the statements or behaviours of various US allies and adversaries are to be appreciated. The importance of these points is made evident later in the same question and answer exchange, when foreign editor Susan Chira responds to a query about whether she was surprised by the content of the leaks:

> The cables give us a deeper understanding of how the United States conducts diplomacy, and a clearer portrait of its allies and enemies. To read the story of how the United States carefully assembled a coalition for harsher sanctions against Iran is to watch diplomacy in action through a lens we seldom see—cajoling here, reassuring there, horsetrading all the way to the end. (Chira 2010)

Clearly, media attention to "scandals" such as Cablegate need not entail any real critique of power. Commentary such as that cited above makes America's alleged role in safeguarding an otherwise precarious global order appear both natural and desirable. Moreover, the presence of debates regarding such matters as whether Julian Assange should be viewed as a hero or a terrorist, whether US spying on allies is inexcusable or sensible, and so on, serves an important rhetorical function, intended or otherwise, for mainstream news outlets like the *Times*. Specifically, it reinforces the image of an open press ready to engage fearlessly with matters of grave concern to the public, even as it masks the propaganda role routinely played by the media on issues where a strong elite consensus exists. This point is particularly critical with respect to global developments of which most citizens have little if any knowledge beyond what they glean from the news media, an issue taken up below with respect to relevant commentary on Iran.

PART II: STATE'S SECRETS LEADING STORY: ARAB PANIC OVER IRAN

The fact that most of the opinion pieces quoted above mention Iran is not coincidental. Leaked statements made by several Arab Gulf State leaders about Iran, along with leaked documents pertaining to that country's alleged purchase of advanced missiles form North Korea, provided the *Times* with its leading story regarding cable content. As previously indicated, less than half of the pieces in the sample dealt specifically with the content of the diplomatic cables and related questions of US foreign policy, 132 in total. However, of these a disproportionate number, 49 of all news pieces in this category, made at least some reference to Iran's nuclear programme. The issue drew heaviest attention during the first week of reporting, when editorializing about the leak was also the most prominent. In addition to making Cablegate a more sensational news event, coverage of this issue fit within a much longer-standing political and media campaign to demonize Iran as a dangerous "rogue state".

Of the articles appearing in State's Secrets approximately 20—plus or minus several guest contributions and "subscribers only" pieces—take the form of editorials or analyses, with most appearing during the first week of coverage. Editorials hold special importance within larger news narratives. They set the general tone for the overall reporting, providing cues and establishing points of reference from which the reader may better appreciate the nature and significance of relevant facts and developments. More specifically with respect to State's Secrets, the general themes identified in Part I merge seamlessly with related commentary about Iran. For example, in a piece by David Brooks entitled "The Fragile Community":

> Despite the imaginings of people like Assange, the conversation revealed in the cables is not devious and nefarious. The private conversation is similar to the public conversation, except maybe more admirable. Israeli and Arab diplomats can be seen reacting sympathetically and realistically toward one another. The Americans in the cables are generally savvy and honest. Iran's neighbors are properly alarmed and reaching out. (Brooks 2010)

Similarly, the previously cited editorial "WikiLeaks and the Diplomats" (Editorial Board 2010a) comments that "the administration has been under pressure from both Israel and Arab states to attack Tehran's nuclear program pre-emptively. It has wisely resisted, while pressing for increasingly tough sanctions on Iran." The critical point here, as it is with the standard reporting on the issue, is that virtually all the editorializing in State's Secrets proceeds from the premise that during the timeframe in question Iran was actively pursuing a nuclear weapons programme and that the US government and intelligence services were deeply concerned about the matter. The reality was very different. The one notable exception in this regard is a guest piece by Rami G. Kouri, then editor-at-large of the *Lebanese Daily Star*. In a contribution entitled "The Sad Loss of National Dignity", Kouri (2010) points out that Arab opposition to Iran is far from universal, and cites the complete lack of proof offered by the Gulf Arab leaders concerning an Iranian nuclear weapons programme.

The opening page of State's Secrets includes two major stories about the alleged nuclear threat posed by Iran. These stories are derived from two distinct sets of documents. The first story, entitled "Around the World, Distress over Iran", is accompanied by a photograph of Iranian President Mahmoud Ahmadinejad standing at the head of a large military assemblage. Beneath it is the caption "Diplomatic cables show how two presidents have dealt with Iran and how President Obama built support for a harsher package of sanctions". The related four-page article quotes King Abdullah of Saudi Arabia who implored Washington to "cut off the head of the snake", that is, Iran, and discusses the fears expressed by other Gulf State leaders regarding Iranian intentions. Linked to it is a map identifying countries where various politicians had made relevant statements in this regard. The main article makes it clear that the leaks in question are newsworthy largely because they appear to confirm what Israel had been saying for decades, but which Arab leaders had been reluctant to express publicly, namely, that Iran's nuclear weapons programme is a menace to the region and must be eliminated.

Predictably, these cable leaks were greeted with great satisfaction by Israeli Prime Minister Benjamin Netanyahu who asserted that "Israel has not been damaged at all by the WikiLeaks publications"; rather, "the documents show many sources backing Israel's assessments, particularly of Iran" (Ravid 2010). Israel is the only state in the Middle East with a known nuclear weapons capability, one dating back to the late 1960s (Hersh 1991). Unlike Iran, however, Israel is not a signatory to the Nuclear Non-proliferation Treaty (NPT). Hence its nuclear activities are not monitored by the International Atomic Energy Agency (IAEA). It is also an occupying power, illegally holding and settling Arab territory captured during the Six-Day War of 1967. Following that war Israel became the leading recipient of US financial and military aid worldwide, a privilege it has enjoyed ever since. Yet, while Israel's fears about Iran are taken seriously in the *Times*, its own substantial nuclear arsenal gets scant notice, receiving only two brief mentions in State's Secrets.

While the Israelis have been agitating for stronger US action against Iran since the early 1990s, American and Gulf State hostility dates to the Iranian Revolution in 1979 when the US lost Iran as a key regional ally (Mearsheimer and Walt 2008). The Arab Gulf monarchies, long propped up by Western governments, feared revolutionary Iran as a powerful state offering an alternative Islamic model of government (Moushabeck 1991). Both the US and the Arab Gulf States supported Iraq when it invaded Iran in 1980, an act which led to an eight-year war. After the US attacked Afghanistan and Iraq in the wake of 9/11, concern grew among US policymakers that Iran's relative power and influence was growing in the region and needed to be held in check. These points suggest that US hostility towards Iran does not stem primarily from the latter nation's intent or potential ability to develop nuclear weapons per se, but rather from American geostrategic interests and related efforts to maintain the dominance of the US and its client states in the oil-rich Middle East.

While the latter possibility is left entirely unexamined in State's Secrets, it helps account for why successive US administrations have consistently worked to isolate and destabilize Iran. It also explains why the US deliberately sabotaged a deal arranged by Turkey and Brazil in 2010, and agreed to by Iran, that would have guaranteed that Iran would never gain nuclear weapons (Porter 2014). As it turned out, the cable leaks supplied new ammunition for those pushing for military action against Iran. The latter included Israel's powerful lobby in Washington and American neo-conservative politicians and think tanks more generally (Mearshimer and Walt 2007; Porter 2014). These were the same elements that led the campaign for the US attack on Iraq in 2003 based on the false charges, endlessly repeated in the mainstream press including the *New York Times*, that Iraq was hiding weapons of mass destruction and that the Iraqi government colluded with Al-Qaeda in the 9/11 terror attacks (Moeller 2004).

As a signatory to the NPT, Iran has the right to develop nuclear power for peaceful purposes (Beeman 2016). Moreover, 19 other non-nuclear weapons' signatories to the NPT enrich uranium just as Iran was doing, and several of these nations had or have indicated that they might have a nuclear weapons programme in the future (Beeman 2016). It is also noteworthy that a religious decree or "fatwa" was delivered by Iran's Supreme Leader Ali Khamenei in 2005 against the development of nuclear weapons (Porter 2014). This followed a similar fatwa from Ayatollah Ruhollah Khomeini in December 1987 against the use of chemical weapons. As Prasad (2015) notes, the earlier ruling is significant because it came after Iraq used chemical weapons, components of which were supplied by the West, against Iranian troops during the Iran/Iraq war. Yet, Iran refrained from retaliating with such weapons, despite its known capacity to produce and deploy them (Porter 2014).

As the discussion so far suggests, at least as important as what is said about the Iranian issue in the American media, is what is left unspoken. It is only when certain relevant facts are brought to light that the propaganda dimension of mainstream news reporting on the issue becomes apparent. The facts in question range from matters of record concerning what the US truly believes about Iran's nuclear ambitions, to more specific information concerning the leaked documents themselves. Most tellingly, not a single article in State's Secrets makes mention of a US National Intelligence Estimate (NIE) from 2007 which states, "We judge with high confidence that in the fall of 2003, Tehran halted its nuclear weapons program" (ODNI 2007). Given the unprecedented nature of the sanctions regime put in place against Iran by the Obama administration, it bears mentioning that another NIE made in 2011 reached the same conclusion as the 2007 estimate.

This omission on the part of the media is hardly minor. Every NIE reflects the consensus of all 17 US intelligence services, and during the timeframe in question the intelligence community was under considerable pressure to find evidence of an Iranian nuclear weapons programme (Beeman 2008; Porter 2014). In fact, there are good reasons to believe that the only time Iran was ever seriously interested in such a programme was when it was closely allied to the US while under the rule of the Shah (Porter 2014, 2018). It is also worth observing that the lack of attention to the 2007 NIE contrasts starkly with the media's more recent behaviour in the wake of Russiagate. Specifically, when WikiLeaks disclosed the contents of emails stolen from the Democratic National Convention (DNC) in 2016, the findings of a conspicuously anaemic, and much less authoritative, National Intelligence Assessment (NIA) became the basis for a full-blown media campaign against Russia for its alleged meddling in the US federal election of that year (see Chap. 6).

The consistent inattention throughout State's Secrets to matters that might cast doubt on Iran's nuclear weapons ambitions extended to outright censorship, a fact that pertains to the second leading article on Iran referred to earlier. The article in question is entitled "Iran fortifies Its Arsenal with the Aid of North Korea" (Broad et al. 2010). It reports that "Iran obtained 19 of the missiles from North Korea, according to a cable dated Feb. 24 of this year". It also states that the missiles "could for the first time give Iran the capacity to strike at capitals in Western Europe or easily reach Moscow". However, as Porter (2010) explains in a piece entitled "WikiLeaks Exposes the Complicity of the Press", these claims were cast into serious doubt in another cable, one which the *Times* agreed not to publish at the request of the Obama administration. The cable in question dates from February 2010 and provides a detailed account of how

Russian specialists on the Iranian ballistic missile programme refuted the US suggestion that Iran acquired missiles that could target European capitals.

As historian Gary Leupp (2015) observes, if most people in the US believe that Iran has a nuclear weapons programme, "they do so because the mainstream media refers to it routinely, as though it were a real thing in the real world". In this respect the editors at the *New York Times* were correct to insist that the cable leaks were not revelatory. Just as the American public "knew" that Iraq was hiding weapons of mass destruction prior to the US invasion of that country in 2003, their initial "knowledge" of the Iranian menace was not something they were likely to have gained from reading State's Secrets. Rather, selective use of WikiLeaks' disclosures by the *Times* merely reinforced a propaganda campaign dating back to 1979, the year when Iranian citizens overthrew a brutal dictatorship supported by the West. It must be conceded, however, that those who followed the *Times* coverage of Cablegate may have gained a greater appreciation for the complex diplomacy, political horse-trading, delicate balancing of interests, and so on, exercised by skilled US diplomats in their attempts to mitigate and contain a threat deemed not to exist by America's own intelligence agencies.

CLOSING COMMENTS

Assange may have had more than one goal in mind when he made the decision to supply major international newspapers with leaked information. For example, as discussed in Chap. 2, he may have been pursuing the anarchist agenda of interfering with the (US) state's ability to function in a normal capacity, exposing its ostensibly secretive and/or corrupt character in the process. Nonetheless, it is also clear that supplying the public with important information in a fashion distinct from that traditionally undertaken by the mainstream news media was a key goal as well, one that fits with Assange's notion of scientific journalism. What this chapter demonstrates is that the availability of leaked information to a major news organization in no way affected the basic ideological character of its reporting on relevant issues. Rather than exposing any deep flaws in the system, the integration of such material into mainstream news discourse served instead to valorize practices of US diplomacy, justifying business as usual on the foreign policy front while underscoring the importance of American world leadership.

Does this mean that WikiLeaks' cooperation with the corporate media was a complete failure? No. In fact, WikiLeaks did achieve one very important goal by working with and/or supplying material to leading news organizations. Not only did the group gain worldwide recognition, but it did so in a way that firmly established its credibility as a reliable source of leaked information. It was noted earlier that the *Times*, and the mainstream media more generally, has often been highly critical of Julian Assange and the organization he represents. The fact remains, however, that the *Times*, *The Guardian*, and so on, repeatedly—as in the cases of the Afghan War Logs, Iraq War Logs and Cablegate—staked their reputations on the authenticity of the information WikiLeaks provided.

When responding to the reader query "are the documents genuine?" *Times* executive editor Bill Keller responds as follows:

> The contents of the cables are consistent with much other reporting we have done on America's foreign relations, and the format is familiar from embassy cables we have seen from other sources. But the most reliable authentication is this: In our extensive conversations with the United States government—in this case, and in the two previous releases of classified documents by WikiLeaks—no official has questioned the genuineness of the material, or suggested that they have been manipulated in any way. (Keller 2010)

The importance of such recognition should not be underestimated. It essentially established WikiLeaks' reputation as the pre-eminent, trusted source for leaked information, a fact which helps explain why no imitator has achieved a similar level of notoriety. The significance of this fact in relation to WikiLeaks' ongoing relevance to the US cultural and political scene will be explored in the remaining chapters of this book.

REFERENCES

Beckett, Charlie, and James Ball. 2012. *WikiLeaks: News in the Networked Era*. Cambridge: Polity Press.

Beeman, William O. 2016. Iran Won the Vienna Accords by Agreeing to Stop What It Never Was Doing. *Huffington Post*, July 17. https://www.huffingtonpost.com/entry/iran-won-the-vienna-accor_b_7821818.html.

Brevini, Benedetta, and Graham Murdock. 2013. Following the Money: WikiLeaks and the Political Economy of Disclosure. In *Beyond WikiLeaks: Implications of Communications, Journalism and Society*, ed. Benedetta Brevini, Arne Hintz, and Patrick McCurdy, 35–55. New York: Palgrave Macmillan.

Broad, William J., James Glans, and David E. Sanger. 2010. Iran Fortifies Its Arsenal with the Aid of North Korea. *The New York Times*, November 28. http://www.nytimes.com/2010/11/29/world/middleeast/29missiles.html.

Brooks, David. 2010. The Fragile Community. *The New York Times*, December 29. http://www.nytimes.com/2010/11/30/opinion/30brooks.html.

Brooks, David, and Collins, Gail. 2010. Have We Learned Anything from the Leaked Cables? *The New York Times*, December 1. https://opinionator.blogs.nytimes.com/2010/12/01/have-we-learned-anything-from-the-leaked-cables/.

Chira, Susan. 2010. Answers to Readers' Questions About State's Secrets. *The New York Times*, November 29. http://www.nytimes.com/2010/11/29/world/29askthetimes.html?pagewanted=all.

Cohen, Roger. 2010. American Diplomacy Revealed—as Good. *The New York Times*, December 2. http://www.nytimes.com/2010/12/03/opinion/03ihtedcohen.html.

Curran, James. 2005. Mediations of Democracy. In *Mass Media and Society*, ed. James Curran and Michael Gurevitch, 122–149. London: Hodder Arnold.

de Vreese, Claes H. 2005. News Framing: Theory and Typology. *Information Design Journal* 13 (1): 51–62. https://msap-unlam.ac.id/download/bahan__bacaan/New%20Framing.pdf.

Editorial Board. 2010a. WikiLeaks and the Diplomats. *The New York Times*, November 29. http://www.nytimes.com/2010/11/30/opinion/30tue1.html.

———. 2010b. A Note to Readers: The Decision to Publish Diplomatic Documents. *The New York Times*, November 28. http://www.nytimes.com/2010/11/29/world/29editornote.html.

Entman, Robert N. 1993. Framing: Toward Clarification of a Fractured Paradigm. *Journal of Communication* 43 (4): 51–58. https://www.unc.edu/~fbaum/teaching/articles/J-Communication-1993-Entman.pdf.

Friedman, Thomas. 2010. We've Only Got America A. *The New York Times*, December 14. http://www.nytimes.com/2010/12/15/opinion/15friedman.html.

Fuchs, Christian. 2014. WikiLeaks and the Critique of the Political Economy. *International Journal of Communication* 8: 2718–2732. http://fuchs.uti.at/wp-content/IJOCWL.pdf.

Gamson, William A., and Andre Modigliani. 1989. Media Discourse and Public Opinion on Nuclear Power: A Constructionist Approach. *American Journal of Sociology* 95 (1): 1–37.

Harshaw, Tobin. 2010. The Hunt for Julian Assange. *The New York Times*, December 3. https://opinionator.blogs.nytimes.com/2010/12/03/the-hunt-for-julian-assange/.

Herman, Edward S., and Noam Chomsky. 1988. *Manufacturing Consent: The Political Economy of the Mass Media*. New York: Pantheon Books.

Hersh, Seymour. 1991. *The Samson Option: Israel's Nuclear Arsenal and American Foreign Policy*. New York: Random House.

Hunt, Albert. 2010. Good Gossip, and No Harm Done to U.S. *The New York Times*, December 5. http://www.nytimes.com/2010/12/06/us/06iht-letter.html.

Keller, Bill. 2010. Answers to Readers' Questions About State's Secrets. *The New York Times*, November 29. http://www.nytimes.com/2010/11/29/world/29askthetimes.html?pagewanted=all.

Kouri, Rami G. 2010. The Sad Loss of National Dignity. *The New York Times*, December 1. http://www.nytimes.com/2010/12/02/opinion/02iht-edkhouri.html.

Leup, Gary. 2015. Talking Points on the Iran Nuke Deal. *Counterpunch*, August 5. https://www.counterpunch.org/2015/08/05/talking-points-on-the-iran-nuke-deal/.

Lynch, Lisa. 2013. The Leak Heard Round the World? Cablegate in the Evolving Global Mediascape. In *Beyond WikiLeaks: Implications of Communications, Journalism and Society*, ed. Benedetta Brevini, Arne Hintz, and Patrick McCurdy, 56–77. New York: Palgrave Macmillan.

McChesney, Robert W. 2008. *The Political Economy of Media: Enduring Issues, Emerging Dilemmas*. New York: Monthly Review Press.

McCombs, Maxwell E., and Donald L. Shaw. 1972. The Agenda-Setting Function of Mass Media. *The Public Opinion Quarterly* 39 (2): 176–187. https://www.researchgate.net/publication/209410047_The_Agenda-Setting_Function_of_Mass_Media.

Mearsheimer, John J., and Stephen M. Walt. 2008. *The Israel Lobby and U.S. Foreign Policy*. London: Penguin Books.

Moeller, Susan. D. 2004. Media Coverage of Weapons of Mass Destruction. A Report for the Center for International and Strategic Studies at Maryland. http://www.pipa.org/articles/WMDstudy_full.pdf.

Moushabeck, Michel. 1991. Iraq: Years of Turbulence. In *Beyond the Storm: A Gulf Crisis Reader*, ed. Phyllis Bennis and Michel Moushabeck, 25–36. New York: Olive Branch Press.

New York Times. 2010. A Note to Readers: The Decision to Publish the Diplomatic Documents. *The New York Times*, November 28. https://www.nytimes.com/2010/11/29/world/29editornote.html.

Office of the Director of National Intelligence. 2007. Iran: Nuclear Intentions and Capabilities. November 2017. https://www.dni.gov/files/documents/Newsroom/Reports%20and%20Pubs/20071203_release.pdf.

Pedro, Joan. 2011. The Propaganda Model in the 21st Century. *International Journal Communication* 5: 1865–1905. http://ijoc.org/index.php/ijoc/article/view/785/666.

Philo, Greg. 2007. Can Discourse Analysis Successfully Explain the Content of Media and Journalistic Practice? *Journalism Studies* 8 (2): 175–196. https://doi.org/10.1080/14616700601148804.

Porter, Gareth. 2010. WikiLeaks Exposes the Complicity of the Press. *Counterpunch*, December 1.

———. 2014. *Manufactured Crisis: The Untold Story of the Iran Nuclear Scare.* Charlottesville: Just World Books.

———. 2018. The Latest Act in Israel's Iran Nuclear Disinformation Campaign. *Consortium News*, May 3. https://consortiumnews.com/2018/05/03/the-latest-act-in-the-israels-iran-nuclear-disinformation-campaign/.

Prasad, Vijay. 2015. Why the Iran Deal Is Essential. *Counterpunch*, August 31. https://www.counterpunch.org/2015/08/31/why-the-iran-deal-is-essential/.

Ravid, Barak. 2010. Netanyahu: WikiLeaks Cables Prove Israel Is Right on Iran. *Haaretz*, November 29.

Stone, Geoffrey R. 2011. A Clear Danger to Free Speech. *New York Times*, January 3. http://www.nytimes.com/2011/01/04/opinion/04stone.html.

CHAPTER 5

Emerging Affinities: WikiLeaks in the Context of a Legitimation Crisis

Abstract Over time, WikiLeaks has adjusted its strategies to take better advantage of a densely populated and globally networked media environment, and the larger reality of an ongoing political legitimation crisis. By directing attention to injustices associated with free trade and the security state, the whistle-blower platform has provided fodder for foreign news operations such as *Russia Today*, progressive alternative platforms like *Democracy Now* and *The Young Turks* and right-wing populist and/or conspiracy-oriented news forums like *Breitbart* and *InfoWars*. In the process WikiLeaks has been able to deliver its message of an ostensibly corrupt and broken political/economic order to divergent audiences in a way compatible with its anarchist agenda.

Keywords Legitimation crisis • Distrust • Media fragmentation • Strategy • Conspiracy theories

> *Side by side with the official myth of a beleaguered government*
> *threatened by riots, demonstrations, and unmotivated, irrational*
> *assassinations of public figures, a popular mythology has taken shape*
> *that sees government as a conspiracy against the people themselves.*
> *(Christopher Lasch 1984, 44)*

© The Author(s) 2018
S. M. E. Marmura, *The WikiLeaks Paradigm*,
https://doi.org/10.1007/978-3-319-97139-1_5

87

In the first four chapters of this book, emphasis was placed on a seeming paradox. On the one hand, WikiLeaks has repeatedly demonstrated its ability to make vast quantities of information formerly kept secret or confidential by powerful institutions accessible to average citizens. On the other, there is little to suggest the emergence of any significant grassroots response to the release of such information in the US. The US case has received special consideration in this book since it is American institutions and policies which have been the targets of WikiLeaks' most sensational disclosures, and hence the national context within which they might be expected to have the greatest impact. Consequently, the implication in much though not all of the previous discussion was that despite its considerable achievements, WikiLeaks may not present any kind of meaningful challenge to the political status quo in the US. In this chapter, I explore an alternative possibility, namely, that Assange's organization has in fact been playing a modest and indirect, but also a cumulative and increasingly detectable role with respect to growing public dissatisfaction with the American political system.

WikiLeaks' capacity to affect media and political discourse in the US was made overt, if only temporarily, during the dramatic run-up to the federal election of 2016, following the group's release of the Democratic National Convention (DNC) emails, and the related "Russiagate" scandal. However, WikiLeaks' relevance to the American political scene has arguably been growing since the major disclosures of 2010/11, even if not conspicuously. This chapter looks at changes to WikiLeaks' targets and strategies since Cablegate, and how these overlap with global political trends, ongoing changes in civil society and the media environment at the local/national level. The main argument I will pursue in this regard is that WikiLeaks' greatest challenge to the political status quo in the US is not based on the possibility that the contents of any one leak will spark mass protest. Nor does it stem from WikiLeaks' ability to enhance the efforts or advance the agenda of any particular activist group or political constituency. Rather, it derives from the organization's unique capacity to contribute to dynamics associated with an ongoing crisis of legitimacy with respect to the political system.

WikiLeaks has refined its ability to exploit key features of the post-truth media environment described in Chap. 2. Moreover, the whistle-blower organization is now well-positioned to exacerbate political dissent in the US for several related reasons, some of which might at first appear contradictory. Foremost among these are the group's established reputation as a credible source of leaked information; its attractiveness as a resource for virtually any identity unhappy with politics as usual; its capacity to thrive in a cultural and political environment marked by growing distrust of dominant institutions, and by the related prevalence of conspiracy theorizing in both mainstream and alternative media forums. Unlike the case with most activist groups and networks, WikiLeaks' agenda and mode of operation need not place it at odds with other elements striving for political change, even as the visions and goals of the latter may differ markedly. It is noteworthy that some of the same factors that limited the group's success early in its career, including its lack of strong roots in American civil society and its troubled relationship with mainstream news organizations, appear to have benefitted WikiLeaks over the longer term.

To better appreciate why, it is necessary to reconsider some of the challenges posed to WikiLeaks over a longer timeframe. This means devoting attention not only to the changing targets and related timing of WikiLeaks' disclosures, but also to the ambivalent space the whistle-blower platform occupies vis-à-vis authoritative knowledge and the competing truth claims of disparate actors. When considered together, these factors help account not only for WikiLeaks' enduring utility as a resource for activists, but also for the affinities the organization appears to share with a broad range of actors in American civil society. Critically, the latter include not only the ostensibly progressive social movements and media forums with which WikiLeaks itself most closely identifies, but also populist elements on the political right. Putting these issues in their proper perspective means approaching them with an eye to the larger context within which WikiLeaks' activities have ultimately come to take on their greatest significance, the global crisis of the nation state.

THE SYSTEM IN CRISIS

In the years following Cablegate, the mood of the American public has proven increasingly volatile. This was made abundantly clear during the Democratic and Republican Party leadership campaigns of 2016. Two populist candidates, Bernie Sanders and Donald Trump, upset the plans and strategies of their own respective parties, straying widely from traditional policy stances and inspiring enthusiasm among broad swaths of the American public. The news media's tendency to focus on Trump's more obnoxious, chauvinistic and anti-immigrant statements and policy positions was coupled with commentary to the effect that Sanders was an idealist whose socialist instincts put him out of touch with hard economic and political realities (Naureckas 2015). These media frames masked an important reality. All questions of their personal sincerity aside, the two candidates were courting supporters largely through appeals to competing versions of economic nationalism, a stance directly at odds with both prevailing global trends and the neoliberal orientation of their own political parties.

While these and other developments surrounding the US federal election of 2016 will receive closer attention in Chap. 6 it is important to flag them here. The relative successes of the Trump and Sanders campaigns reflected popular frustration with larger economic and political trends, themselves tied to a global crisis of political legitimacy. While this crisis has not affected all states or affected all states and regions in the same manner, the larger pattern is clear enough. As Castells (2013, 286–287) documents, the stark reality today is that most citizens the world over, including those living within advanced democracies, do not trust their governments or believe that they reflect the general will and interests of the people. In fact, there has been a steady trend in this regard since the end of the Second World War, reflected in widespread perceptions of governmental and institutional corruption. Political parties, the police and the judicial/legal system are perceived as the most corrupt institutions in society. Significantly, political parties top the list with roughly 70% of the world's citizens viewing them as the most tainted (Castells 2013, 287). The importance of these points in relation to WikiLeaks' activities since Cablegate will be returned to shortly.

The concept of a "legitimation crisis" was first articulated by Jurgen Habermas (1975) in a work of the same name. Habermas used the concept to describe a situation in which the dominant institutions of ostensibly democratic, capitalist, state societies are no longer viewed by the general population as embodying their collective will or as reflecting their true values and interests. The original focus of Habermas's analysis was on "welfare state" or Keynesian capitalism, the version that gained prominence during the two decades following the Second World War. Habermas contends that under the welfare model problems of governmental legitimacy arise due to the increasing displacement of the norms, moral outlook and sources of motivation which underpinned an earlier phase of capitalist development. His arguments in this regard are much like those developed by Bell (1976) concerning the "cultural contradictions" of capitalism. Both theorists underscore the deepening penetration, or for Habermas "colonization", of grassroots culture by capital. As mass markets for consumer goods become increasingly saturated, the creation of ever more consumer "needs" vis-à-vis advertising and marketing is necessary to offset potential crises of production. This in turn encourages a hedonistic culture of consumption directly at odds with the Protestant work ethic of frugality, self-discipline and deferred gratification that once spurred economic innovation and productivity (Plant 1982, 344).

The state's role is also at issue. It was the growing instability of capitalism as it reached its monopoly phase, combined with circumstances wherein state, society and economy were relatively localized and coextensive, that both necessitated and allowed for an increasingly intrusive, regulatory role on the part of governments. In the case of welfare capitalism, the state must regularly intervene to address potential imbalances of supply and demand and adjust markets in a manner which benefits the entire economy, and not merely the interests of any one industry, sector or competitor. The administrative, rationalistic logic informing the state's actions is similar in character to that guiding decision-making within large-scale, bureaucratized capitalist institutions. As Habermas (1989) argues, both state and corporate bureaucracies are geared towards purely instrumental ends, administrative efficiency and profit-making, respectively. The modes of communication and decision-making operating within such institutions therefore contrast sharply with those that give rise to cultural norms and values within the "lifeworld" of inter-subjective social experience. With respect to the authority of the state, the upshot is that its right to regulate the economy, as with its increasing role in managing other aspects of peoples' lives, is not always self-evident in the eyes of the citizenry. In fact, the state cannot help but take on the appearance of an intrusive outside force, manipulating markets and other aspects of society in technocratic fashion. Hence, its regulatory policies and other governing practices must in some way be legitimized (Habermas 1975).

In the case of the welfare state, legitimacy hinges upon the state's ability to demonstrate that its policies serve the general interests of its citizens (Calhoun 1992, 30). Traditionally, this has meant the provision of universal social goods such as education, healthcare, basic infrastructure, social security, job-training, and so on. The state also gains legitimacy through its role as arbiter and legal guarantor of compromises achieved when the demands of labour and those of industry appear irreconcilable. For Habermas, the resulting status quo is flawed in key respects. This is because the state's actions serve to obscure the contradictions inherent in capitalism, forestalling the type of collective deliberation needed to clearly identify common interests and create a more genuinely democratic and representative society (Calhoun 1992). Similarly, social tensions arising from such matters as class and racial inequality and the domination of the political establishment and public sphere by elite interests continue to persist. Nonetheless, for several decades the welfare state model remained relatively successful and stable. Governments were at least somewhat responsive to pressures from the electorate, and not only from industry. Additionally, considerable control over the domestic economy and a related ability to create a stable tax base allowed government to distribute resources in a manner which enabled a relatively high standard of living for the majority.

During the 1970s, both the institutions and ideological bases of the welfare state began to come under sustained assault. At that time, politicians and economists in the US were seeking solutions to the problem of "stagflation", economic stagnation combined with rampant inflation (Harvey 2005). The proposed solution came in the form of neoliberalism, which entailed the shift to an allegedly more laissez-faire style of capitalism. However, under the new neoliberal model the state appears less well-equipped to stave off a crisis of legitimacy. This is primarily because any explicit ideological commitment to the general welfare of the public has been dispensed with (Harvey 2005). The state's new role is simply to create conditions optimal for unrestricted commerce, in line with the dubious premise that ultimately the majority will benefit as a result. The related notion that neoliberalism represents a return to a more pristine style of capitalism, creating opportunities for anyone possessing the right values and commitment to entrepreneurial innovation and achievement, is also problematic. Today the global economy is dominated by financial institutions and business conglomerates largely immune to competition from small players. Furthermore, these conglomerates often bear little or no allegiance to the state societies from which they operate, a fact not lost on a growing portion of citizens around the globe.

The rise of the global economy over roughly the past four decades has led to an accompanying loss of economic sovereignty on the part of states (Castells 1996, 1997). One consequence is that today the prospects of American citizens along with countless others around the globe are increasingly shaped by far-reaching trade agreements such as the General Agreement on Tariffs and Trade (GATT), the North American Free Trade Agreement (NAFTA) or more recently the (formerly) anticipated

Transatlantic Trade and Investment Partnership (TTIP) and Transpacific Partnership (TPP). Such agreements, which have received broad bipartisan support in the US, take precedence over the domestic laws of participating states. They are also negotiated behind closed doors by figures largely unknown to the public, their true nature and scope remaining obscure. Moreover, the prominence of transnational corporations, and the regulatory power of international monetary and trade institutions such as the International Monetary Fund (IMF) and the World Trade Organization (WTO) has created a new reality in which power and politics are splitting apart. As Bauman and Lyon (2013, 5) observe, while politics remains local, "power now exists in global and extraterritorial space".

Within the US, these trends have been reflected in various ways. The reduction of the welfare state has been met with an increasing consolidation of the security state, a point to be returned to shortly. There has also been a steady decline of organized labour, once an important pillar of the Democratic Party. As Green Party candidates such as Ralph Nader and Jill Stein have often emphasized, this decline has led to a situation where the two traditional political parties have become increasingly beholden to essentially the same collection of powerful corporate and financial interests. This situation was exacerbated in 2010 when the US Supreme Court, in the case of *Citizens United* vs. *Federal Election Commission*, ruled that government may not prohibit unions and corporations from making independent expenditures for political purposes. These developments are consistent with the findings of a study by Gilens and Page (2014) suggesting that while economic elites and organized groups representing business interests have substantial independent impact on US government policy, average citizens and mass-based interest groups have little or no independent influence.

In the years since Cablegate, WikiLeaks has worked diligently to draw attention to precisely such realities. For example, between 2013 and 2015 the organization conducted staggered releases of secret transcripts from the TPP trade deal negotiations, a subject given further attention below. WikiLeaks' efforts in this regard overlapped in terms of its general timing with two other major leaks, namely, the Panama Papers leak and those made by Edward Snowden concerning the mass state surveillance programme known as PRISM. While both disclosures took place independently of WikiLeaks, they placed the spotlight on related problems of global inequality and changing state priorities. This was most obvious in the case of the Panama Papers leak of April 2016. It included

11.5 million files from the database of Mossack Fonseca, the world's fourth largest offshore law firm, dwarfing even WikiLeaks' disclosures of 2010/11. Obtained from an anonymous source by the German newspaper *Süddeutsche Zeitung*, which later shared them with *The Guardian*, the BBC and the *New York Times*, the leak drew widespread attention to the ways in which the rich may exploit secretive offshore tax havens (Harding 2016).

I do not intend to discuss the Panama Papers leak in any detail here, but simply wish to stress its relevance to the global crisis of political legitimacy referred to above. For example, the leak revealed that 12 national leaders were among 143 politicians, their families and close associates from around the world known to have been using offshore tax havens (Harding 2016). The fact that most, though by no means all, of the activity documented in the leak was technically legal is largely beside the point. What matters is that the leak came at a time when widespread perceptions of an unfair system were already high. As Colin Holtz reported in *The Guardian*, the leak made clear that "if the super-rich actually paid what they owe in taxes, the US would have loads more money available for public services" (Holtz 2016). In the US, vast disparities of advantage are often blamed by right-wing populists on "crony capitalism", whereby the rich benefit from a rigged, but otherwise virtuous system. In the case of the left, the problem is more likely to be viewed as rooted in capitalism itself, or at least in the unwillingness of politicians to reign in its excesses. However, when the institutions of the state are perceived as beholden to finance, the target of public anger, that is, a corrupted political and economic system, is essentially the same, even when the ideologies of those agitating for reform are not. More will be said on this shortly.

The changing priorities of the state under the conditions of neoliberal globalization were brought to the public's attention from a rather different angle in 2013. Edward Snowden, then a contractor for the National Security Agency (NSA), leaked the existence of the massive surveillance programme known as PRISM to the *Washington Post* and *The Guardian*. PRISM represents only the latest phase of the US government's post-9/11 electronic surveillance efforts. Like similar programmes before it, PRISM allowed for the gathering of mass amounts of personal data from the Internet and phone correspondence of millions of Americans. In theory, such mega-data may then be analysed to identify anomalies that could lead to the apprehension of terrorists or identify other security threats. More than WikiLeaks' revelations of 2010, the existence of this programme struck a chord with both the mainstream media and the public. While the extreme secrecy surrounding such programmes make assessments of both their legality and their effectiveness problematic, the Snowden leak did inspire considerable debate about surveillance and privacy. In contrast to Assange, much of the mainstream media attention given to Snowden has been sympathetic. Nonetheless, like Assange, Snowden felt compelled to seek refuge, in this case in Russia, to avoid prosecution under the US Espionage Act of 1917.

With respect to concerns about corporate and surveillance practices more generally, the American public has often appeared apathetic or slow to perceive such practices as a serious threat to civil liberties (Marmura 2010; Solove 2007). But public concern about state surveillance, which today invariably involves the active or passive cooperation of corporate entities like Bell, Google, Facebook, Microsoft, and so on, is growing, and has gained increasing attention from journalists. In fact, one important outcome of the Snowden leak was the creation of a new online media outlet, the *Intercept*, by Glenn Greenwald, Laura Poitras and Jeremy Scahill. In addition to housing the files associated with this and other leaks, the online journal has a similar social justice orientation to that of WikiLeaks. While it has sometimes provided criticism of WikiLeaks and its leader, it has generally defended the organization, including its disclosure of the DNC emails in 2016. Overall, the media outlet is best conceived of as an ally of WikiLeaks, one likely to increase the latter organization's profile, rather than as a hostile rival. It is also one of the WikiLeaks new "media partners". The importance of such partners and of other closely related developments are addressed below.

A MANY-HEADED HYDRA

Numerous researchers have stressed the growing importance of participatory media within the global attention economy, a reality that provides opportunities as well as challenges for activists. For example, Tufekci (2013) points to the increasing visibility of "microcelebrity activists", nonestablishment personalities associated with various political causes. She argues that the latter have often proven able to punch above their weight in terms of influencing mainstream media discourse. Similarly, Bimber (2003) maintains that in the American context, the advent of Internet technology has created conditions whereby the traditional boundaries and structures of organizations now exert much less influence over who has facility with political information and communication, and by extension the ability to address and organize publics. The idea that the Net may benefit at least some small media players relative to those associated with the established political older holds considerable importance here, particularly given WikiLeaks' potential capacity to reinforce the rhetorical power of diverse and often competing grassroots activists simultaneously. It also holds relevance when reconsidering WikiLeaks' lack of deep roots in American civil society, and the difficulties the organization experienced during its early attempts to distribute leaked information.

It is worth recalling the fallout from WikiLeaks' fateful decision in 2010 to share information with the *New York Times* and other leading newspapers. Despite clear failures in terms of exploiting the revelatory potential of leaked material through such cooperation, WikiLeaks did manage to establish itself as the most widely recognized and ostensibly reliable source for authentic leaked information. In a time of declining public trust in powerful institutions, this is a critical asset indeed. Moreover, WikiLeaks' critics in the mainstream media must tread carefully. Insofar as the activist group continues to be perceived as credible by those on the political margins or who otherwise consider its revelations important, attacks upon it appear at least as likely to increase suspicion of WikiLeaks' detractors as of the whistle-blower organization itself. The dynamics become more complex when politicians and major news outlets take opposing sides on the matter of leaking as they did during Russiagate. For now, it is enough to address the reality that in the years since Cablegate, an increasing number of activist groups and alternative media outlets have not only come to treat WikiLeaks as credible, but also to make regular use of its resources.

When WikiLeaks began leaking transcripts from the TPP negotiations in 2013, it did so not only on its own website and through the distribution of an extensive series of videos and interviews on YouTube, but also with the aid of countless other small and large media providers both domestically and internationally. The latter included players from across the political spectrum, ranging from left-wing environmental and global justice activists to "alt-right" nationalist organizations opposed to the emerging "new world order". This was a reflection both of a new strategy on WikiLeaks' part and of genuine popular hostility towards the TPP and other state and corporate policies closely tied to economic globalization. Turning first to WikiLeaks' own efforts, Lynch (2013) documents that following publication of the Cablegate material by its initial media partners, namely, the *New York Times, The Guardian, El Pais, Le Monde* and

Der Spiegel, WikiLeaks engaged in a determined effort to build up an international network of new media partners. The fruits of these efforts are advertised on *WikiLeaks.org*, where it is affirmed that the organization now has "contractual relationships and secure communications paths to more than 100 major media organizations from around the world".

WikiLeaks' more notable foreign media partners include Russia Today (RT). Intriguingly, the station claims to be the most popular foreign news network in seven of the largest cities in the US, putting it ahead of the BBC and Al Jazeera America in those markets (Shuster 2015). RT devoted extensive airtime to coverage of the TPP leak, including numerous interviews with Julian Assange on the matter. Even earlier, in 2012, the station allowed Assange to host his own show, "World Tomorrow", described on *WikiLeaks.org* as "a collection of twelve interviews featuring an eclectic range of guests, who are stamping their mark on the future: politicians, revolutionaries, intellectuals, artists and visionaries". Much like Al Jazeera, especially during its early years, RT is frequently denounced by Western politicians and media outlets as an anti-US propaganda platform and was even designated a hostile foreign agent in the wake of Russiagate. Its critics include *Guardian* writer Luke Harding (2012) who described Assange as a useful idiot for the Kremlin, a charge to be repeated later by Democrats following the leak of stolen DNC emails by WikiLeaks in 2016. However, such partnerships and the inevitable criticism they provoke from some fit with WikiLeaks' ongoing attempts to address diverse audiences through multiple media pathways simultaneously.

WikiLeaks' strategy of cultivating new media partners anticipates the fact that while some news operations may be averse to writing about particular leaks or parts of leaks, outlets in other countries or those with different political leanings will be more likely to do so, or might frame the same issues very differently. For example, Lynch (2013, 60) notes that despite having a broad geographic range, WikiLeaks' early partners like the *New York Times* and *The Guardian* produce news primarily with an elite European or North American audience in mind. As such they reflect "historic patterns of imperial or neo-imperial news flows", a reality underscored in Chaps. 3 and 4 of this book. Hence, while a major American news partner might be unenthusiastic about highlighting negative aspects of trade deals pushed by powerful interests in their own country—and which exclude participation by Russia and China—RT has no such scruples. The point is not that foreign or alternative media outlets are invulnerable to top-down pressures—RT is funded by the Russian state—or might not reflect strong biases or agendas of their own. Rather, WikiLeaks' strategy incorporates the logic of triangulation whereby, ideally at least, leaked material is distributed not only to news organizations in different regions, but also to those with opposing political views (Lynch 2013, 61).

At least as importantly, within the US context WikiLeaks' strategy has been mirrored by a similar dynamic emerging from the bottom up. It was noted in Chap. 2 that WikiLeaks once tried to encourage crowdsourcing or otherwise locate elements within the public capable of interpreting and distributing leaked information at the grassroots level. It was also observed that this strategy was abandoned early on as impracticable. However, the civil society conduits WikiLeaks sought but failed to identify or cultivate early in its career appear to have coalesced over time, even if not always in ways likely to have been anticipated by the activist group. Today, WikiLeaks is both reported upon and utilized by a multitude of activists and alternative news outlets in the US, many of which now act as inter-mediaries and interpreters of political events for their respective publics, putting out newsletters online or hosting their own programmes on YouTube. Some of these have grown to become a substantial presence on the web with enormous followings. I will comment only on some of the more noteworthy examples in this chapter, largely to illustrate two points. First, that the groups or news outlets in question tend to focus on issues closely linked to the political crisis of legitimacy outlined above. Second, and related to the last point, some of the most enthusiastic users and/or defenders of WikiLeaks come from the populist right as well as the anti-establishment left.

The most natural allies and supporters of WikiLeaks are arguably those closely associated with what is often referred to as the global justice movement, namely, anarchist and/or socialist leaning groups and individuals overtly opposed to neoliberalism and the growing inequalities with which it is associated at both the global and national levels. For example, Castells (2012) suggests that in terms of both its outlook and its mode of opera-tion WikiLeaks holds natural affinities with what he refers to as the new "networked social movements", non-hierarchical activist networks in which the technical and communicative skills of individuals like Assange often play a critical role. Castells (2012, 221) is referring primarily to the wave of social movement activity spurred by the global economic crisis of 2008. He emphasizes that this crisis threatened countries as well as major corporations with economic collapse. It also led to further assaults on the welfare state "on which social stability had been predicated for decades".

The protest activism in question occurred throughout 2009–2012 and included the "kitchenware revolution" in Iceland, itself sparked by financial corruption in that country's banking sector, the Arab Spring uprisings, the Indignados or anti-austerity movement in Spain, and the Occupy movement that emerged in Washington DC before it spread globally.

These movements overlapped with and learned from one another and hence should be viewed as both local and global in orientation (Castells 2012). As Castells (2012, 223) puts it "they express an acute consciousness of the intertwining of issues and problems for humanity at large, and they clearly display a cosmopolitan culture, while being rooted in their specific identity". It is also worth recalling that as noted in Chap. 3 in the case of the Arab Spring, "hacktivist" groups like Anonymous and WikiLeaks have at times provided direct assistance to such protest movements, for example, by helping them circumvent state or corporate efforts to thwart their communications (Milan 2013). The main concern here, however, is with the sympathetic coverage that WikiLeaks regularly receives from progressive media outlets advancing similar social justice or public interest agendas. They, like WikiLeaks, are highly critical of growing corporate power and its influence over the two main political parties in the US. Many such outlets have proven sympathetic to WikiLeaks over time and were also at the forefront of publicizing leaks about the TPP. Moreover, they report on WikiLeaks' disclosures in much the same way the organization had originally striven for, namely, in a manner highly critical of dominant economic and political institutions.

A prominent example is *Democracy Now*, an independent news organization hosted by Amy Goodman and Juan Gonzalez. Beginning as a radio programme in 1996, it is now a highly popular news show on the web and is currently pioneering the largest public media collaboration in the US. The station consistently reports on anti-corporate global activism, particularly since the Seattle protests of 1999 against the WTO, and gave full coverage of the TPP leaks. Its mission includes giving citizens and grassroots activists a voice and/or the opportunity to debate with establishment figures. *Democracy Now* also provides an important venue for Green Party candidates like Jill Stein, and plays a vigorous watchdog role with respect to US foreign policy. It also continues to provide WikiLeaks with an important platform, something it has done consistently since the major leaks of 2010, but without the disparagement WikiLeaks often receives from mainstream news outlets including its initial news partners.

Another progressive news outlet openly sympathetic to WikiLeaks is *The Young Turks* (TYT). This network presently hosts the most widely watched news programme on YouTube, surpassing even major corporate media giants like CNN, MSNBC and FOX in terms of audience share (Blattberg 2014). Its founder and CEO Cent Uygur was a former employee of MSNBC who grew disenchanted with the mainstream news media's establishment orientation. Perhaps best associated with the traditional or moderate American left, Uygur and others at TYT have championed the need for a renewal of the Democratic Party. The station has been a harsh critic of the "corporate coup" in America and has repeatedly denounced Democratic politicians for their alleged pseudo-progressivism and subservience to finance. Like *Democracy Now*, the station was a harsh critic of the TPP, and drew repeated attention to WikiLeaks' disclosures on the issue. It also denounced Hillary Clinton's early support of the trade deal and praised Bernie Sanders's rejection of it. The station has also proven to be a consistent defender of WikiLeaks.

Given their public interest and citizen empowerment orientation, it is perhaps unsurprising that alternative news outlets such as the *Intercept*, *Democracy Now* and TYT have been both sympathetic to WikiLeaks and eager to report on its disclosures. However, WikiLeaks' appeal now extends well beyond the left, and has grown to include groups and individuals who frequently emphasize the need to transcend older divisions of right/left politics or who have extensive audiences on the anti-establishment right. Perhaps the most notorious example is *Breitbart News*, an outlet frequently in the spotlight due to its consistent support for Donald Trump and its wide popularity with the alternative or "alt-right". The latter term is frequently used to refer to ultra-nationalist groups and individuals that include but are not restricted to anti-Semitic and racist elements. Its former CEO Steve Bannon once served as the Trump White House Senior Strategist. Significantly, *Breitbart*'s extensive references to WikiLeaks go beyond an interest in the DNC emails, a topic taken up in the next chapter, but also reflect the outlet's hostility to free trade agreements and its fears concerning the machinations of the "deep state".

It is interesting that Assange appears satisfied with the fact that WikiLeaks has proven useful to those on the populist right as well as to left-wing activists. This issue will receive further attention in Chap. 6. In the meantime, it should be emphasized that as with the case of left-wing anti-corporate activism, the growth of the alt-right in the US is also linked to economic globalization on the neoliberal model. As noted earlier, national economies, once largely contained and managed by the state, have become increasingly embedded in global markets. Habermas refers to the fallout of these developments in Europe as follows:

> The trends summed up in the word 'globalization' are not only jeopardizing, internally, the comparatively homogeneous make-up of national populations – the prepolitical basis for the integration of citizens into the state – by prompting immigration and cultural stratification; even more tellingly, a state that is increasingly *entangled* in the interdependencies between the global economy and global society is seeing its autonomy, capacity for action, and democratic substance diminish. (Habermas 1998, 398)

Habermas's statements seem prophetic with respect to developments such as BREXIT, Namely, Britain's exit from the European Union. This development was driven at least as much by the growing influence of populist nationalism in England as it was by left-wing opposition to the power of global capital. Moreover, expressions of economic nationalism and hostility to immigration are growing throughout Europe, not only in countries hard hit by austerity measures like Greece and Spain, but also in economically prosperous nations like France and Germany. Similar resentments towards a perceived new world order are increasingly visible in the US. Economic disruptions closely associated with free trade agreements such as NAFTA have resulted not only in a shrinking white middle class, but also in increasing flows of immigrants, including mass legal and illegal immigration, across America's southern border (Bacon 2017). As in Europe, such developments have provoked considerable anxiety, often manifesting itself in expressions of outright xenophobia and racism. This reality has been exploited adeptly by Republicans like Donald Trump and Ted Cruz. As Harvey (2005) emphasizes, in the absence of other strong bases of collective solidarity, exaggerating both internal and external threats is a particularly useful means of shoring up popular support.

As the welfare functions of the state become increasingly privatized, devolving to the individual and community level, the state itself becomes deemphasized as a source of collective identity and moral authority (Castells 1997). Rising expressions of ultra-nationalism in the US therefore dovetail with the state's ongoing attempts to justify its highly aggressive foreign policy. While it has not fought a defensive war since the Second World War, the US continues to be involved in direct military operations in Afghanistan, Iraq and Syria, and periodically or indirectly in many other countries including Ukraine, Libya, Pakistan, Yemen, Columbia and Lebanon. As emphasized in Chap. 3, the propaganda which necessarily accompanies such interventions, including a related lack of mainstream media attention to anti-war protests, has made it difficult for the anti-war left to break out of its own media bubble to address the broader public. Nonetheless, in recent years even the efficacy of wartime propaganda as a means for shoring up political legitimacy appears to be losing some of its usual potency.

It is significant that during his election campaign Donald Trump adopted an "isolationist" foreign policy stance at odds with the aggressive interventionism advanced by neoconservatives within his own party. And when he declared that US military involvement in Iraq had proven to be a "complete disaster" for America, his message went over well with a constituency not typically associated with anti-war activism. Trump was essentially reminding his supporters that war is expensive. Adopting blunt nativist rhetoric, and appealing largely to disaffected white voters, he made the case that fewer resources should be devoted to foreign "nation-building" with more efforts directed towards creating infrastructure and providing better opportunities at home. My argument here is not that the anti-war left and nationalist right are moving closer ideologically. The important point is that the US political system faces growing challenges from the public that the core policies of both the Republican and Democratic Parties appear ill-equipped to address. The fact that Trump felt compelled to adopt a more interventionist foreign policy stance once he was elected, one institutionalized by successive Republican and Democratic administrations since the Second World War, merely underscores this point. WikiLeaks thrives in the present political environment precisely because it provides ready ammunition to the political system's rapidly multiplying chorus of critics.

CONSPIRACY AS GOVERNANCE

As emphasized in previous chapters, Assange views his organization as a journalistic enterprise, one necessitated by the failure of mainstream news organizations to carry out their self-proclaimed watchdog role by providing a meaningful check on the abuse of power. Similarly, in terms of its commitment to social justice and greater democratization, WikiLeaks appears to share much in common with left-wing activists hoping to reform the Democratic Party and/or with those calling for the establishment of more publicly oriented and independent news media organizations. However, both WikiLeaks' mode of operation and related arguments made by Assange to justify WikiLeaks' existence and activities also suggest a more subversive and ostensibly anarchist agenda, one that goes beyond a simple commitment to reformist politics. As Fenster (2012, 778) observes, Assange's statements and theories, which sometimes appear to be in conflict, combine Habermasian ideals of an informed citizenry and vibrant public sphere with a more radical technological threat to disrupt the authoritarian state.

In his short essay *Conspiracy as Governance*, as well as in comments made in numerous other contexts, Assange (2006) makes it clear that he views the apparatuses of political and economic power dominant in the world today as essentially conspiratorial in character. Put differently, he considers contemporary systems of governance as working largely independently of any public knowledge or input. At the level of state power, this reality is reflected not only within regimes typically understood as authoritarian such as North Korea, Syria or Russia, but also within Western liberal democracies such as Britain, Australia or the US. Similarly, the mainstream media in these countries are viewed as part and parcel of the same conspiratorial order. The important point here is not that most members of the public who have heard about or even consulted WikiLeaks are likely to have read Assange's commentary on these matters. What is significant is that the worldview informing WikiLeaks' agenda not only resonates strongly with a diverse range of actors in American civil society but is also reflective of the general mood of the times.

Debate continues as to the main contributors to a growing "conspiracy culture" in America, one wherein radicalized suspicion towards messages originating from sources formerly deemed authoritative is matched by credulity towards alternative accounts of reality unamenable to confirmation or debunking (Andrejevic 2013). The most important factors behind this growing phenomenon, and to growing distrust of authority more generally, are arguably structural in character, linked both directly and indirectly to the global crisis of political legitimacy described in this chapter. This point is important when considering the additional appeal, beyond its utility as a resource, that WikiLeaks holds to a diverse array of actors upset with the political status quo. Despite a high level of diversity and unpredictability with respect to the specific content of its disclosures, WikiLeaks has managed to convey one key message consistently over time. As suggested above, the message, sometimes implicit and sometimes explicit, is

that the prevailing political order is essentially conspiratorial and unac-
countable, geared primarily to its own survival rather the good of its
citizens.

If there is a common thread tying the rising distrust of the state that
began during the post-war period of welfare state capitalism to that which
exists at even greater intensity under the conditions of neoliberalism, it is
arguably the experience among citizens of an increasing loss of control
over the circumstances most directly affecting their lives. As Lasch (1984,
44) emphasizes, "angry citizens who find themselves living near poison-
ous chemical dumps or nuclear power plants, neighbors who band together
to keep out schools for retarded children or low-income housing or nurs-
ing homes, angry taxpayers, opponents of abortion, opponents of housing, and minority groups all see themselves, for different reasons, as victims
of policies over which they have no control". Moreover, they increasingly
view themselves as oppressed not only by bureaucracy, big government
and opaque technological systems, that is, by the technocratic forces
referred to earlier by Habermas in conjunction with the welfare state, but
also by "high level plots and conspiracies involving organized crime, intelligence agencies, and politicians at the upper reaches of government"
(Lasch 1984, 44).

Given that WikiLeaks' very existence signifies governmental and corporate secrecy, it seems fitting that the organization is both regularly cited
and heavily defended in Alex Jones's highly popular *Info Wars* and *Prison
Planet* news sites on YouTube. Perhaps America's most notorious conspiracy theorist, Jones was and remains an outspoken proponent of the
"Truther" claim that 9/11 was an "inside job". On his various news programmes Jones discusses and promotes a wide range of conspiracy theories
involving "big pharma", alleged world government attempts to control
the food supply, gun control, population control, secret weapons experi-
ments, and so on. Intriguingly, and despite his ongoing support for
Donald Trump, Jones regularly cites the need to move beyond right/left
distinctions in politics. Much like the 9/11 Truth Movement he helped
inspire, Jones's website and conspiratorial mode of analysis tends to blur
the causes and concerns one might associate with groups like the Tea Party
on the one hand and Greenpeace or Occupy on the other. Hence, in addition to the threats allegedly posed by a government determined to disarm
its citizens and foment race wars—*Info Wars* does not promote racism but
regularly refers to alleged divide and rule plots invoking race by various
powerful conspirators—Jones's news programmes also devote considerable

airtime to diatribes against free trade, genetically modified organisms and the machinations of the corporate media.

A similar mindset informs commentary on *Off the Grid*, a YouTube news channel hosted by former professional wrestler, Minnesota Governor and host of the TV show "Conspiracy Theory", Jesse Ventura. Like fellow Truther Alex Jones, Ventura was an ardent opponent of the TPP agreement, referring to the related WikiLeaks material in a series of YouTube videos devoted to the topic. Ventura was also incensed by disclosure of the PRISM programme, hailing Edward Snowden as an American hero and interviewing the whistle-blower's legal advisor Ben Wiesner on his programme. Ventura is an admirer of libertarian politician Ron Paul, himself an ardent defender of both Snowden and Assange. Like Ron Paul, Ventura fears the power of the security state and advocates similar libertarian ideals of individual and communal self-sufficiency. He also deeply distrusts the existing two-party political system and has interviewed other critics of establishment politics on his programme including Cenk Uygur of TYT. His book *DemoCRIPS and ReBLOODlicans: No More Gangs in Government* (2012) calls for replacing the present system with one of independent candidates.

It is significant that the networked conspirators referred to in Conspiracy as Governance are not imaginary, even if the language Assange employs encourages a misleadingly agential conception of power. As Castells (2012, 7) emphasizes, global financial networks and global multimedia networks are intimately linked, creating a meta-network holding extraordinary power. And in a time when media constitute the space of politics, ready access to communication networks is key for all contenders. Hence, counterpower must be networked to be effective, a reality that explains both why governments fear the Internet and why corporations try to use it to extract profit while limiting its potential for freedom (Castells 2012). Neither the logic of communicative capitalism nor the capacity of powerful interests to disseminate propaganda on a vast scale could ever be entirely circumvented by activists utilizing alternative media. However, as an organization challenging existing arrangements of power, WikiLeaks stands out. Rather than representing only one among many competing identities, each largely communicating within its own media/identity network, WikiLeaks' subversive potential stems largely from its demonstrated ability to reinforce lines of propaganda and/or political critique within media outlets utilized by elements advancing disparate political outlooks simultaneously.

In the latter respect at least, WikiLeaks appears well adapted to a post-truth regime, one wherein those identified as belonging to various issue-publics or truth markets are encouraged to ascribe authority to their own media, believe their own conspiracy theories, demonize their specific enemies, and so on. WikiLeaks continues to be viewed with suspicion by much of the American public, a reality that places limits on its effectiveness as a form of counterpower. Yet, the whistle-blower platform need not be popular for its influence to be felt. Working through multiple conduits, it enhances expressions of dissent that resonate within disparate, competing segments of the population. To the extent that the latter may never be entirely contained or redirected by market forces, WikiLeaks necessarily contributes, even if only modestly, to the larger crisis of political legitimacy described in this chapter. Consequently, when WikiLeaks began releasing the DNC emails in 2016 it was well-positioned to influence both mainstream and alternative political discourse in the US. By the same token, it was inevitable that WikiLeaks would again become a major propaganda target, this time for its alleged cooperation with a hostile foreign power. These issues are explored in the remaining chapter of this book.

REFERENCES

Andrejevic, Mark. 2013. *Infoglut: How Too Much Information Is Changing the Way We Think and Know*. New York/London: Routledge.

Assange, Julian. 2006. Conspiracy as Governance. *me @ iq.org*: 1–4. http://nakamotoinstitute.org/static/docs/julian-assange-conspiracies.pdf.

Bacon, David. 2017. NAFTA, The Cross-Border Disaster. *The American Prospect*, November 7. http://prospect.org/article/nafta-cross-border-disaster.

Bauman, Zygmunt, and David Lyon. 2013. *Liquid Surveillance*. Cambridge: Polity Press.

Bell, Daniel. 1976. *The Cultural Contradictions of Capitalism*. New York: Basic Books.

Bimber, Bruce. 2003. *Information and American Democracy*. Cambridge: Cambridge University Press.

Blattberg, Eric. 2014. The Young Turks Is Running Circles Around News Networks on YouTube. *Digiday*, October 31. https://digiday.com/media/the-young-turks-interview/.

Calhoun, Craig. 1992. Introduction: Habermas and the Public Sphere. In *Habermas and the Public Sphere*, ed. Craig Calhoun, 1–50. Cambridge: MIT Press.

Castells, Manuel. 1996. *Rise of the Network Society*. Oxford: Wiley-Blackwell.

————. 1997. *The Power of Identity*. Oxford: Wiley-Blackwell.

————. 2012. *Networks of Outrage and Hope*. Cambridge: Polity Press.

————. 2013. *Communication Power*. 2nd ed. Oxford: Oxford University Press.

Fenster, Mark. 2012. Disclosure's Effects: WikiLeaks and Transparency. *Iowa Law Review* 97: 753–807. https://ssrn.com/abstract=1797945.

Gilens, Martin, and Benjamin I. Page. 2014. Testing Theories of American Politics: Elites, Interest Groups, and Average Citizens. *Perspectives on Politics* 12 (3): 564–581. https://doi.org/10.1017/S1537592714001595.

Habermas, Jurgen. 1975. *Legitimation Crisis*. Trans. Thomas McCarthy. Boston: Beacon Press.

————. 1989. *Lifeworld and System: A Critique of Functionalist Reason*. Trans. Thomas McCarthy. Boston: Beacon Press.

————. 1998. The European Nation-State: On the Past and Future of Sovereignty and Citizenship. Trans. Ciaran Cronin. *Public Culture* 10: 397–416. https:// read.dukeupress.edu/public-culture/article-abstract/10/2/397/31543/ The-European-Nation-State-On-the-Past-and-Future.

Harding, Luke. 2012. The World Tomorrow: Julian Assange Proves a Useful Idiot. *The Guardian*, April 17. https://www.theguardian.com/media/2012/ apr/17/world-tomorrow-julian-assange-wikileaks.

————. 2016. What Are the Panama Papers? A Guide to History's Biggest Data Leak. *The Guardian*, April 5. https://www.theguardian.com/news/2016/ apr/03/what-you-need-to-know-about-the-panama-papers.

Harvey, David. 2005. *A Brief History of Neoliberalism*. Oxford: Oxford University Press.

Holtz, Colin. 2016. The Panama Papers Prove It: America Can Afford a Universal Basic Income. *The Guardian*, April 8. https://www.theguardian.com/com- mentisfree/2016/apr/07/panama-papers-taxes-universal-basic-income-pub- lic-services.

Lasch, Christopher. 1984. *The Minimal Self: Psychic Survival in Troubled Times*. New York: W.W. Norton & Company.

Lynch, Lisa. 2013. The Leak Heard Round the World? Cablegate in the Evolving Global Mediascape. In *Beyond WikiLeaks: Implications of Communications, Journalism and Society*, ed. Benedetta Brevini, Arne Hintz, and Patrick McCurdy, 56–77. New York: Palgrave Macmillan.

Marmura, Stephen. 2010. Security Vs Privacy: Media Messages, State Policies, and American Public Trust in Government. In *Surveillance, Privacy and the Globalization of Personal Information*, ed. Elia Zureik, Lynda Harling Stalker, Emily Smith, David Lyon, and Yolande Chan, 100–126. Montreal/Kingston: McGill-Queen's University Press.

Milan, Stefania. 2013. WikiLeaks, Anonymous and the Exercises of Individuality: Protesting in the Cloud. In *Beyond WikiLeaks: Implications of Communications,*

Journalism and Society, ed. Benedetta Brevini, Arne Hintz, and Patrick McCurdy, 85–100. New York: Palgrave Macmillan.

Naureckas, Jim. 2015. NYT Suggests Sanders Is 'Unelectable' for Siding with Majority on Tax Hikes for Rich. *FAIR*, July 1. https://fair.org/home/nyt-suggests-sanders-is-unelectable-for-siding-with-majority-on-tax-hikes-for-rich/.

Plant, Raymond. 1982. Jurgen Habermas and the Idea of Legitimation Crisis. *European Journal of Political Research* 10: 341–352. https://onlinelibrary.wiley.com/doi/abs/10.1111/j.1475-6765.1982.tb00029.x

Shuster, Simon. 2015. The Global News Network RT is the Russian Government's Main Weapon in an Intensifying Information War with the West—and Its Top Editor Has a Direct Phone Line to the Kremlin. *Time*, March 5. http://time.com/rt-putin/.

Solove, Daniel. 2007. 'I've Got Nothing to Hide' and Other Misunderstandings of Privacy. *San Diego Law Review* 44 (289): 745–772. https://papers.ssrn.com/sol3/papers.cfm?abstract_id=998565.

Tufekci, Zeynep. 2013. "Not This One": Social Movements, the Attention Economy, and Microcelebrity Activism. *American Behavioral Scientist* 57 (7): 848–870. http://journals.sagepub.com/doi/abs/10.1177/0002764213479369.

Ventura, Jesse. 2012. *DemoCRIPS and ReBLOODlicans: No More Gangs in Government*. New York: Skyhorse Publishing.

CHAPTER 6

Wikileaks' American Moment: The DNC Emails, Russiagate and Beyond

Abstract WikiLeaks' disclosure of stolen Democratic National Convention (DNC) emails in 2016 and the related "Russiagate" scandal had tangible implications for US politics. These events draw attention to the evolving relationship(s) between state propaganda, populist conspiracy theorizing and mainstream news reporting. The proliferation of alternative information sources complicates attempts to verify relevant claims about WikiLeaks and/or Russia. In addition to the competing conspiracy theories promoted by fringe elements, major news organizations like MSNBC and FOX increasingly tailor their news products to satisfy different truth markets. WikiLeaks has proven resilient in the face of ongoing attempts to discredit it. However, its future success hinges not only on its media skills and strategies but also on developments and contingencies beyond its control.

Keywords DNC emails • Russiagate • Propaganda • News • Conspiracy theories • Truth markets

It was during the run-up to the federal election of 2016 that WikiLeaks most clearly demonstrated its capacity to affect the character of political and media discourse in the US. This was not just a case of the group providing fodder for yet another major news scoop or media spectacle. The whistle-blower platform proved able, and in a dramatic way, to exploit an ongoing political legitimation crisis and influence national

© The Author(s) 2018   109
S. M. E. Marmura, *The WikiLeaks Paradigm*,
https://doi.org/10.1007/978-3-319-97139-1_6

politics in the process. Through its disclosure of leaked Democratic National Convention (DNC) emails, WikiLeaks cast doubt not only on the willingness of the DNC to back a candidate offering meaningful policy alternatives to those of the Republican Party, but also on the organization's integrity as a democratic institution. By the same token, the DNC leak provoked the wrath of much of the political and media establishments, cementing the resolve of WikiLeaks' enemies to destroy the organization's reputation as a trustworthy source of authentic, leaked information. An intense propaganda campaign, one inseparable from the ensuing "Russiagate" scandal, was undertaken with the aim of discrediting both WikiLeaks and the Trump administration for their alleged ties to Moscow. And in a further, related twist, WikiLeaks found itself with allies in such unlikely quarters as FOX News.

These and related developments are addressed in this chapter, building on the discussion and arguments put forward in Chap. 5. Attention is devoted to WikiLeaks' role in exacerbating the legitimacy problem already facing both major political parties, to the activist group's witting and unwitting participation in a conspiracy theory and propaganda war among competing establishment and fringe actors, and to how mainstream news outlets such as MSNBC and FOX attempted to exploit public divisiveness and popular anger to better engage their respective truth markets. These issues are in turn tied to consideration of WikiLeaks' ability to weather the storm of criticism levelled at it by its detractors. While the group's longevity and future success are of course impossible to predict, I argue here that WikiLeaks has again proven resilient in the face of serious adversity, and that its reputation as a credible source of leaked information will survive Russiagate. Moreover, while the anti-democratic tendencies associated with a post-truth media environment will likely endure for the foreseeable future, it appears probable that despite the challenges it faces WikiLeaks will continue to navigate that same environment skilfully while providing a valuable resource for activists.

In the months leading up to the federal election of 2016, the global crisis of political legitimacy described in Chap. 5 was not only highly visible in the US but it also appeared to be coming to a head. It was Democratic hopeful Bernie Sanders and Republican contender Donald Trump who were best prepared to respond to this crisis, and who proved the most adept at tapping into populist anti-establishment and anti-elite sentiments. What these two candidates promised, or at least appeared to promise, was a revitalization or remaking of their own parties from within. Despite enormous differences in their political philosophies and programmes, both Sanders and Trump signalled their willingness to undertake major policy shifts that appealed to growing numbers of Americans. The latter included reining in free trade and reducing the offshoring of jobs, curbing the influence of powerful lobbyists and providing greater access to affordable healthcare. In addition, both candidates appeared more reluctant than did challengers from within their own parties to continue the type of interventionist foreign policy long pursued by Republican and Democrat administrations alike.

Above all, Trump and Sanders managed to gain large-scale public support in the face of determined opposition from within the upper ranks of their respective party establishments, and from powerful financial backers of both parties. This despite ongoing demonization and ridicule—or in Sanders's case, prolonged inattention—from the mainstream news media (Patterson 2016). Throughout 2016, both contenders defied the expectations of pundits and analysts, drawing enormous crowds of enthusiastic supporters to their rallies and embarrassing the candidates preferred within their own party establishments. Of greatest relevance here, Bernie Sanders was riding a growing tide of popular support, particularly among youthful voters, highlighting the discrepancy between the strong support Hillary Clinton enjoyed from party delegates versus the more even split of voters favouring either Clinton or Sanders among the Democratic base. It was against this backdrop that on July 22, 2016, WikiLeaks released the first of 44,053 emails and 17,761 attachments stolen from the DNC, the governing body of the Democratic Party. This was soon followed by the release of emails taken from the personal Gmail account of Clinton's campaign chairman John Podesta in October and November of that year.

While the email correspondence in question dealt with a range of sensitive issues, revelations in two related areas stood out. These spoke to the heart of the crisis of political legitimacy and associated resentments described in the previous chapter, striking a chord with much of the public. The first and most fateful of these concerned email exchanges indicating that the DNC was intentionally sidelining Bernie Sanders to ensure that Hillary Clinton would lead her party and ultimately claim the presidency. This included an email from a DNC staffer advocating a press strategy whereby the Sanders campaign could be portrayed as inept and in disarray. Other correspondence indicated that the day before Clinton's March 13 CNN Town Hall debate against Sanders, interim DNC Chair Donna Brazile had passed relevant questions to the Clinton campaign in advance. DNC officials also discussed ways to exploit Sanders's potential vulnerability on faith questions. The idea was that by outing Sanders as an atheist as opposed to an observing Jew, he would lose support among religious Christian voters.

The second most damaging aspect of the leak concerned Clinton's ties to "big money". It seems clear that even before the leak, Sanders's supporters viewed the self-proclaimed Social Democrat as a more genuinely left-wing and/or progressive candidate than his rival. Sanders had already criticized Clinton's close ties to Wall Street, rhetoric that appealed to his growing following of youthful voters. Remarkably, a poll taken on the eve of the Iowa caucuses indicated that more than 40% of likely Democratic caucus attendees self-identified as socialists (Meyerson 2016). In any event, Sanders's image as the more left-leaning choice was surely reinforced when transcripts of Clinton's triple digit speeches to Goldman Sachs were made public by WikiLeaks. As Confessore and Eder (2016) wrote in the *New York Times*, an outlet generally sympathetic to Clinton, the DNC leak revealed the "transactional exchanges necessary to harvest hundreds of millions of dollars from the party's wealthy donor class" and captured a world "where seating charts are arranged with dollar totals in mind, where a White House celebration of gay pride is a thinly disguised occasion for rewarding wealthy donors and where physical proximity to the president is the most precious of currencies".

Making matters worse for the DNC, numerous polls suggested that Sanders stood a better chance of defeating Donald Trump in a federal election than did Clinton (Johnson 2016). As discussed in Chap. 5, growing public disenchantment with a political system widely perceived to be in the grip of powerful special interests is a problem that plagues both major parties. A piece in the *Times* by Trip Gabriel (2016) headed, "The More Donald Trump Defies his Party, the More His Supporters Cheer" captured the dynamic at work within the Republican camp. Similarly, while most loyal Clinton supporters likely understood the content of the disclosed emails in terms of politics as usual, for many others the leak could only have reinforced the growing perception that the Democratic establishment had all but abandoned its traditional concern with the interests of ordinary working Americans. The salient point here is that growing numbers of voters appeared eager for candidates prepared to depart from conventional policy stances. The DNC leak thus made the contrast between Clinton and Sanders sharper, contributing to the latter candidate's growing appeal to undecided Democrat-leaning voters (Cassidy 2016). And as many of his supporters recognized, had Sanders received more coverage from mainstream news outlets his chances of leading the Democratic Party would almost certainly have increased (Patterson 2016, 11).

At least as importantly, the leak provided the Trump campaign with a new and potent weapon against the Democrats, one epitomized by Donald Trump's repeated references to "crooked Hillary". The DNC leak had followed on the heels of another scandal that had already damaged the Democrats. In March 2015, it became publicly known that during her tenure as Secretary of State, Hillary Clinton had used her private family email server for official communications rather than using the official State Department accounts maintained on federal secure servers. The "Clinton emails" included over 100 messages containing classified information at the time they were sent, as well as nearly 2100 that were not marked classified but would retroactively be ranked as such by the State Department. While WikiLeaks played no direct role in this scandal, it did make the Clinton emails available to the public on its website, a fact often cited by those accusing Assange of pursuing a personal vendetta against Hillary Clinton dating back to Cablegate. The efforts made by various parties to demonize WikiLeaks will receive further attention shortly. Here, it is sufficient to point out that taken together these two email scandals put enormous pressure on the Clinton campaign to formulate an effective strategic response.

The necessary ammunition arrived on Oct 7, 2016, when the Office of the Director of National Intelligence (ODNI) and the Department of Homeland Security (DHS) issued a joint statement to the effect that the US intelligence community was confident that the Russian government had directed recent hacking of emails with the intention of interfering with the US election process. Later, on January 6, 2017, the ODNI released a National Intelligence Assessment (NIA), "Assessing Russian Activities and Intentions in Recent US Elections", affirming that the Russian military intelligence service had hacked the servers of the DNC and the personal Gmail account of Clinton campaign chairman John Podesta before passing their contents along to WikiLeaks (ODNI 2017). The NIA also asserted that the hacking attempt was part of a broader campaign ordered by Russian President Vladimir Putin, aimed at hurting Hillary Clinton's chances of winning the election. The fallout from these reports soon became known as Russiagate, a landmark political scandal involving an ongoing investigation into the Trump administration's alleged ties to the Kremlin, and a related campaign to discredit WikiLeaks and other foreign and alternative media sources as hostile "foreign agents".

At the time of writing, the true nature of the events behind Russiagate and the long-term implications of this historic scandal are far from clear. Considerable fog still surrounds the ongoing investigation into the business and political dealings allegedly involving either Donald Trump or his close associates on the one hand and Russian businesses and political interests on the other. Many claims of illicit activity refer to undertakings that date back over many years and, assuming they are well-founded, may have little if any connection to the events surrounding the 2016 election. Likewise, while some evidence of election meddling, such as the existence of Russian "troll factories" and related ads and posts on social media, now appear to be well established, numerous other accusations against Russia that gained public attention through mainstream news reports were later found to be unsubstantiated. Crucially for present considerations, questions remain as to whether WikiLeaks did in fact receive the DNC emails from Russian agents, a charge flatly denied by Julian Assange.

Directly related to the points above, a longer-term trend is visible in the US whereby practices of mass communication once associated with political deliberation in peacetime have increasingly taken on the character of communication strategies deployed during times of war (Harsin 2006, 85). It is a development that mirrors America's shift to a permanent war footing, a situation Paul Virilio and Sylvere Lotringer (1997) famously referred to as "pure war". While perhaps best exemplified by the open-ended War on Terror, it is a process that began following the Second World War. Politicians and military strategists concluded that any future conflicts would have to be fought with whatever military resources were on hand at the outbreak of hostilities, since there would not be time to transform a peace economy onto a war footing (Haggerty 2005, 251–252). Drawing on Virilio's work, Walsh and Barbara (2006) observe that the merging of the Internet with traditional mass media has eroded conventional boundaries of time and geography while multiplying the sources of information available to citizens. They note further that while these conditions ostensibly represent a challenge to the state's authority and legitimacy, they may also provide the state with political cover behind which it can pursue its more aggressive foreign policy goals (Walsh and Barbara 2006).

The relevance of these points is apparent when considering the case of Russiagate. News coverage of this imbroglio is strongly reminiscent of that preceding the US invasion of Iraq in 2003. At that time Americans were bombarded with false or misleading information concerning Iraqi weapons of mass destruction (WMDs) and connections to Al-Qaeda. Similarly, and regardless of the actual level or significance of Russian interference in the 2016 election, most major US news outlets were quick to join politicians in a chorus of anti-Russian rhetoric based on intelligence claims unaccompanied by proof or verification, reminiscent of the case of Iraq. In this sense at least, the role played by the news media vis-à-vis Russiagate transcends partisan disputes, reflecting a broader state interest in mobilizing hostility to Putin's Russia. In recent years, Russia has directly challenged US foreign policy goals in Ukraine, Syria and elsewhere, and appears determined to reassert itself as a power on the global stage. Its attempts to forge deeper economic and political alliances with China and increase its influence through institutions such as BRICS and the Shanghai Cooperation Council have been a source of growing concern to Republicans and Democrats alike. However, as with the Monica Lewinsky scandal that haunted former President Bill Clinton, Russiagate has polarized public opinion. Some well-known conservative commentators, including Rush Limbaugh and Sean Hannity of FOX News, have rallied to President Trump's defence.

Somewhat ironically given the history of the two main political parties, it has primarily been Democrats that have recently adopted rhetoric reminiscent of the Cold War period. At a time when the buildup of US and NATO forces on Russia's borders has reached unprecedented levels, Trump is frequently referred to as a "Kremlin puppet", and WikiLeaks as a tool of Russian intelligence. However, many in the Republican and intelligence establishments also appear eager to be rid of Trump, and/or to prevent any attempts by the President to normalize relations with Russia. By contrast, Trump's populist base, along with FOX News and alternative right-wing outlets like *Breitbart* and *Infowars*, continues to defend the President, dismissing the charges against him as part of a witch-hunt designed to distract attention from the corruption and ineptitude of the Democratic Party. Meanwhile, some popular alternative news sources to the left of Clinton Democrats, including TYT and *The Intercept* (see Chap. 5), have adopted a sceptical attitude towards accusations of high-level Russian interference in the 2016 election, and have also defended WikiLeaks' disclosure of the DNC emails. Given the intense and often confusing nature of the resulting information warfare, it is useful to proceed further not only by considering mainstream news coverage of the

DNC and Russiagate scandals, but also by revisiting the closely related issue of conspiracy theorizing discussed in Chap. 5.

Scholarly debates about the causes and consequences of "conspiracy theorizing" have long been complicated by recognition of the fact that conspiracy theories sometimes turn out to be well-founded (Bratich 2008). Public distrust in dominant institutions is grounded in a genuine crisis of political legitimacy. The DNC's attempts to undermine the Sanders campaign highlight the importance of both these points. In the months preceding the leak, those suggesting that the DNC was biased in Clinton's favour were often ridiculed as conspiracy theorists. Meanwhile, dominant news outlets like the *Times* suggested that Sanders's "radical" policies made him unelectable (Naureckas 2015). DNC officials were clearly aware of the suspicions of Sanders supporters. In late May, three weeks before the critical California primary, a DNC staffer emailed Communications Director Luis Miranda, "Wondering if there's a good Bernie narrative for a story, which is that Bernie never had his act together, that his campaign was a mess." The message ends with the statement "It's not a DNC conspiracy, it's because they never had their act together".

As I have argued elsewhere (Marmura 2014), the readiness with which growing numbers of citizens are prepared to embrace spurious conspiracy theories—and sometimes legitimate ones—cannot be fully appreciated without attention to the relationship between top-down expressions of propaganda and mainstream news production. While it is typically alternative, web-based information sources that are condemned as the progenitors of "fake news", it must also be recognized that legacy news organizations may contribute to public acceptance of conspiracy theories in at least two ways. First, they often provide reinforcement for conspiracy theories either originating within or encouraged and exploited by actors closely linked to the political establishment. These typically take the form of what Ellul (1965) termed agitation propaganda, namely, the type designed to encourage public hostility towards some designated enemy of the state. The Bush administration's successful efforts to link Saddam Hussein's Iraq to the 9/11 terror attacks is one example. Attempts by influential individuals within the Republican Party to encourage beliefs about President Obama's alleged foreign birth, secret Muslim identity and/or links to the Muslim Brotherhood constitute another.

The news media may also be implicated in conspiracy theorizing in a second, less direct but related fashion. When dominant news narratives fail to account for worrisome developments or policies in a sufficiently critical or coherent manner, people may seek out alternative explanations that they find more satisfactory. It should come as little surprise that many Americans refuse to believe that most global trade agreements are negotiated with the best interests of ordinary workers in mind, or that unending US military interventions in places like Iraq, Libya and Syria—which have proven a boon to jihadist groups—are driven primarily by a concern with fighting terrorism. Yet, as discussed earlier, mainstream news organizations often avoid engaging in lines of analyses likely to call such rhetoric into question, especially in cases where a strong elite consensus in outlook is present (Philo 2007). This reality is often obscured by the fact that major news outlets may be willing to circulate ungrounded but sensational claims less likely to invite flak. The salient point here is that at least some members of the public will inevitably feel compelled to search for more satisfying accounts of reality concerning politically sensitive issues than those provided by the likes of ABC, CNN and FOX News.

It is here that the growing importance of the Internet comes into play, exacerbating the problems referred to above. Alternative sources of information online are always at hand to provide explanations for events that, regardless of their veracity, appear more convincing to many than those provided by the mainstream media. The very structure of the web, combined with the countless number of "information providers" utilizing cyberspace, now guarantees that alternative accounts of any given reality are all but inexhaustible. As Dean (2002) emphasizes, the nagging sense that the truth is always both just around the corner, and yet somehow forever out of reach, is itself fed by reliance on a medium in which hypertexts branch off and cross-sect endlessly, offering limitless iterations of any given version of events. It is also the case that the idiosyncrasies and fears of Internet users are monitored and cultivated to advance the interests of commercial media organizations vis-à-vis the identification and manipulation of truth markets. By the same token, the implosion of the new media and mass media environments has put traditional news organizations under relentless pressure to hold viewer/reader attention, and hence to locate and report scoops quickly. These realities in turn encourage news outlets to be less cautious when selecting choice pieces of information, the origins and authenticity of which are often difficult to verify (Harsin 2006, 87).

The contemporary hybrid media environment is one that gives conspiracy theories, rumours and hoaxes a unique circulatory power, and hence the opportunity to be exploited for political purposes (Harsin 2006,

87). This was apparent throughout 2016. As Zeynep Tufekci (2016) relates in a contribution to the *New York Times*, conspiracy theories about the physical and mental health of Hillary Clinton were rampant throughout her campaign. During her recovery from pneumonia, Clinton's frequent coughing fits fuelled speculation on social media that she was experiencing health problems ranging from Parkinson's disease and epilepsy, to advancing dementia. These rumours were in turn linked to the notion that Clinton was able to conceal her frailties because the head of her Secret Service detail was both her hypnotist and a medical doctor. Tufekci (2016) notes that such stories received a boost when Mayor Rudolph W. Giuliani of New York, an ardent Trump supporter, stated on FOX News that the news media had failed to cover Clinton's health, advising viewers to "go online and put down 'Hillary Clinton illness,' take a look at the videos for yourself".

As Harsin (2006) emphasizes, a crisis of verification represents the most salient and politically dangerous aspect of a rumour, and one that poses a serious challenge to journalists.

This is most apparent when journalists are forced to rely solely on official sources for information. While something may or may not be the case, official sources insist that it is (Harsin 2006, 87). This is precisely the predicament facing journalists in the wake of Russiagate. Recalling the naiveté of the press prior to the 2003 invasion of Iraq, Matt Taibbi (2016) of *Rolling Stone* magazine expresses frustration that in the absence of independent verification, reporters must rely upon the secret assessments of intelligence agencies to cover the story at all. He states that "many reporters I know are quietly freaking out about having to go through that again. We all remember the WMD fiasco. 'It's déjà vu all over again' is how one friend put it." Similar misgivings are expressed by Robert Parry of *Consortium News*. While conceding that Russian agents may have hacked the DNC server, Parry (2017) argues that "we don't know the truth and neither does the *New York Times* – and likely neither does the US government". The sentiment is shared by former Iraqi weapons inspector Scott Ritter (2017), who contends that most of those reporting on Russiagate "have chosen to ignore the lessons of Iraq".

In the case of the present news crisis, problems of verification derive from both the nature and the content of the intelligence report which led most major US media outlets to treat the alleged Russian hack of the DNC emails as an established fact. First, while it has routinely been presented as such—the *Times* did not retract its own misrepresentation of the issue until June 29, 2017—the report in question did not take the form of a National Intelligence Estimate (NIE). NIEs are generally considered authoritative because they are based on a consensus among all 17 US intelligence services. By contrast, the Russia NIA did not represent such a consensus, nor was it the product of careful coordination between the CIA, NSA and FBI as is widely understood. Analysts from the three agencies were involved in the NIA's production. However, as former DNI James Clapper testified before a Senate Judiciary subcommittee on May 8, 2016, "the two dozen or so analysts for this task were hand-picked" for the job. Specifically, they were part of a separate, secretive task force operating under the close supervision of the CIA Director, and not as an integral part of their home agency or department (Ritter 2017).

Second, the NIA provides no solid evidence that the DNC email server had been hacked by Russian agents. As Scott Shane (2017) of the *New York Times* wrote, missing from the report is "hard evidence to back up the agencies' claims that the Russian government engineered the election attack". Rather, as Shane (2017) notes, the message from the agencies essentially amounts to "trust us". Most journalists, including others at the *Times*, have chosen to ignore this reality, a noteworthy trend given the admission of the assessment's authors that their judgements "are not intended to imply that we have proof that shows something to be a fact". Moreover, and as emphasized by Herman (2017), rather than presenting evidence of serious Russian election interference, the NIA is largely devoted to defaming the reporting practices of the Russian news network Russia Today (RT). The main thrust of the assessment is that numerous actors were involved in Russian efforts to influence the election in Trump's favour. These included covert intelligence operatives as well as "Russian Government agencies, state-funded media, third-party intermediaries, and paid social media users or 'trolls'" (ODNI 2017). Significantly in this regard, Russian operatives were not accused of interfering with the vote tally, but rather with illicitly procuring damaging documents and then using them to support an "influence campaign".

Both the character and strength of the allegations against Russia deserve careful consideration. If history is any guide, efforts by powerful countries to influence one another's domestic politics are best understood as an ongoing, if unfortunate feature of relations among nation states. Certainly, the US engages in such activity on a regular basis, ranging from routine spying operations, to cyber-warfare, to supporting coups and insurgencies. To cite one recent example, a WikiLeaks disclosure from February 16,

2017, revealed that during the seven months leading to France's 2012 presidential election all major French political parties were targeted for infiltration by the CIA's human ("HUMINT") and electronic ("SIGINT") spies (WikiLeaks 2017a). The US has also interfered in Russian national politics. The July 1996 issue of Time magazine boldly announces covert US efforts to ensure that Boris Yeltsin won the Russian election against his Communist rival. Far from denouncing such activity, the featured article, entitled "Rescuing Boris: The Secret of how four US advisors used polls, focus groups, negative ads and all the other techniques of American campaigning to help Boris Yeltsin win", openly celebrated its success declaring, "Democracy triumphed – and along with it came the tools of modern campaigns, including the trickery and slickery Americans know so well. If those tools are not always admirable, the result they helped achieve in Russia surely is" (Kramer 1996).

I raise these points not to illustrate the hypocrisy of condemning foreign interference in US politics, but simply to underscore the propagandist nature of the media campaign being waged against Russia. Given both the ongoing and ubiquitous nature of information warfare among nation states, and the murky character of the charges levelled against Russia in the Jan 6 NIA, the subsequent behaviour of the mainstream media is striking. As Patrick Lawrence observes in a piece in *The Nation* (discussed further below) the evolution of public discourse in the year following the release of the July 6 NIA is "worthy of scholarly study". As he states, "Possibilities became allegations, and these became probabilities. Then the probabilities turned into certainties, and these evolved into what are now taken to be established truths" (Lawrence 2017). In like vein, Glenn Greenwald of *The Intercept* (2017a) draws attention the credulity and enthusiasm with which numerous accusations of Russian meddling have been greeted by major news outlets, only to be debunked shortly thereafter. They include the headline-making claim that Russia attempted to hack into the voting stations of 21 states, the charge made in the *Washington Post* that Russia had hacked the US electricity grid, a story carried by *The Slate* that Trump had created a secret server with a Russian bank, a *Guardian* story asserting that WikiLeaks had a long relationship with the Kremlin and the suggestion in *Fortune* that RT had hacked into and taken over C-SPAN's network.

One incident that stands out concerning alleged Trump/Russia/WikiLeaks collusion occurred on Friday, Dec. 8 2017, when CNN announced that WikiLeaks had secretly offered the Trump campaign special access to the DNC emails on September 4, 2016. This was ten days before the whistle-blower platform allowed access to the material online. As it turned out, the email in question was really dated September 14, after WikiLeaks had made the emails public (Greenwald 2017b). Later, when compelled to retract the story, CNN claimed that it did not possess the email in question and that "multiple sources" had provided it with the false date. The same pattern occurred in the cases of CBS and MSNBC. CBS News claimed that it had independently confirmed CNN's story and published its own article discussing the grave implications of the discovered collusion. And in the case of MSNBC, "intelligence and national security correspondent" Ken Dilanian also claimed independent verification of the false report. As Greenwald (2017b) put it, Dilanian "spent three minutes mixing evidence-free CIA claims as fact with totally false assertions about what his multiple 'sources with direct knowledge' told him about all this".

Greenwald (2017a) cites many other cases of similar news sourcing practices. For example, he refers to an article in the *Times* dealing with "Russian bots" replicating "anti-American messages" on Twitter, noting that the story is based on information provided by a group called the Alliance for Securing Democracy. Greenwald observes that the recently formed organization, which comprises neoconservatives such as Bill Krystal, along with former acting CIA chief Mike Morell, and Bush Homeland Security Secretary Mike Chertoff, never declares its methods for deciding which Twitter accounts are Kremlin loyal, or for determining what constitutes anti-Americanism. Such examples appear even more noteworthy when one considers the long history of attempts by US intelligence agencies to utilize major news outlets for political purposes. As Boyd-Barrett (2004, 436) documents, this once included the publication of hundreds of books aimed at undermining the Soviet Union and communism, aided by CIA ownership of dozens of newspapers and magazines worldwide. In 1977 it was revealed that over 400 US journalists had been employed by the CIA for over 25 years, with almost every major US news organization penetrated by the CIA at some level. This included Associated Press, ABC, CBS, Hearst Newspapers, *Miami Herald*, Mutual Broadcasting System, NBC, *New York Herald Tribune*, the *New York Times*, *Newsweek*, Reuters, *Saturday Evening Post*, Scripps-Howard, *Time/Life* and United Press International (Boyd-Barrett 2004, 436).

Examples of anti-Russian sentiment in the mainstream media such as those cited above do not mean that Russia did not attempt to interfere in the US election, or that many of the allegations made against it may not be true. The important point here is that the media's zeal to demonize Russia, Trump and/or WikiLeaks cannot be adequately accounted for through reference to the weight of evidence available during the time period in question. It is, however, consistent with the more general interest of competitive news organizations in obtaining scoops, combined with a long-standing and well-documented tendency to uncritically accept claims widely backed by establishment interests, even when the evidence supporting such claims may be weak, suspect or simply lacking (Philo 2007; McChesney 2008). These points matter because as was the case during the Iraqi WMD scare when the public was being prepared for an illegal war, the media's more recent behaviour enabled a significant propaganda achievement. Whether or not the Trump administration ever intended to normalize ties with Russia, the successful campaign has made it all but impossible. And, as Herman (2017) adds, "evidence free claims of a Russian Hacking intrusion have helped divert attention from the real electoral abuses disclosed by the WikiLeaks material".

As previously suggested, it remains unclear whether Russian agents really did hack the DNC email server and then forward its contents to WikiLeaks as claimed in the NIA. A piece by Patrick Lawrence that appeared in the respected left-leaning publication *The Nation* deserves special attention in this regard. Entitled "A New Report Raises Big Questions About Last Year's DNC Hack", the article focuses on the research findings of an organization known as Veteran Intelligence Professionals for Sanity (VIPS). The latter group was formed in 2003 by a collection of 30 former US intelligence officers with decades of experience working within the CIA, the FBI, the NSA and other agencies (Heuvel 2017). As the editor's prelude to the article states, VIPS previously produced some of the most credible analyses of the Bush administration's mishandling of intelligence data in the run-up to the 2003 invasion of Iraq (Heuvel 2017). Significantly, the forensic investigation the group undertook came to radically different conclusions than those reported in the NIA. Most critically, the group claimed that on July 5, 2016, information from the DNC computers was not hacked, but rather leaked by someone with physical access to the DNC's system and then doctored in such a manner as to leave "Russian fingerprints" on the stolen documents.

Given the ongoing and opaque nature of the events surrounding Russiagate, it would be unwise to accept the VIPS findings as the final word on the matter of the stolen DNC emails. In fact, since the time of its publication other qualified investigators, including some dissenting members of VIPS, have taken issue with the report's claim that the leak could only have been an inside job (Heuvel 2017; Urchill 2017). Nonetheless, the VIPS study, and Lawrence's article in *The Nation* concerning it, holds importance here for several reasons. First, most of those behind the investigation continue to stand by its main findings. And well into 2018, much of its plausibility derived from the fact that the US intelligence community had yet to provide hard evidence of Russian involvement. The authors of the VIPS report contend that given the NSA's blanket coverage of the Internet, they should be able to produce evidence of a Russian hack if it exists, noting further that historically the US has disclosed classified information when it has suited its purposes (Binney, et al. 2017). Second, it provides an alternative account for how WikiLeaks obtained the DNC emails consistent with Assange's position that they were not turned over to it by Russia.

Finally, regardless of the validity of the findings it reported, *The Nation* article was quickly seized upon by numerous alternative media ranging from right-wing outlets eager to defend the President, such as *Breitbart* and *Infowars*, to progressive and/or left-wing news sources such as *The Intercept, Counterpunch* and TYT that continue to express scepticism towards many of the official claims made against Russia. This development was of course predictable, fitting with the dynamics of media fragmentation referred to throughout this book, whereby the proliferation of dissenting views is encouraged even as the regime of post-truth described by Harsin (see Chap. 2) is arguably reinforced. Indeed, when highlighting the importance of qualifying their study's conclusions, some VIPS members warned that "the environment around Trump, Russia, et al. is hyperpolarized right now, and much disinformation is floating around, feeding confirmation bias, mirroring and even producing conspiracy theories" (Drake et al. 2017). Adding oil to the fire, the VIPS findings and some other alternative accounts of the stolen DNC emails appeared to be reinforced—at least for some—by information made available by yet another WikiLeaks revelation, one already made public on March 7, 2017.

The leak in question concerned "Vault 7", the code name for the CIA's vast hacking arsenal, which includes a broad range of malware, viruses, trojans and malware remote control systems, along with related documentation. WikiLeaks claim it was able to gain access to this material because the CIA had lost control of it. According to the WikiLeaks web page, the archive "appears to have been circulated among former US government hackers and contractors in an unauthorized manner, one of whom has provided WikiLeaks with portions of the archive" (WikiLeaks 2017b). When providing relevant background, *WikiLeaks.org* refers to the origins of the CIA's hacking division, which began to take shape after 2001 and eventually had over 5000 registered users. The scale of the CIA's undertaking was so vast that by 2016 its hackers had utilized more code than that used to run Facebook (WikiLeaks 2017b). The page states further that the "extraordinary collection" in question gives its possessor the entire hacking capacity of the CIA. This includes a tool known as "Marble". As Lawrence (2017) notes, Marble may be used to mount false flag operations whereby the origin of documents may be obfuscated, while leaving incriminating markings pointing wherever the CIA desires.

As emphasized in the previous discussion, the many uncertainties surrounding the true extent and nature of Russian meddling in the US election of 2016 did not prevent most major news outlets from reflexively adopting the official line that any such interference was both deep and unprecedented. Russiagate also paved the way for the exploitation of rival truth markets. In the case of major corporate news outlets, it was arguably MSNBC that most aggressively catered to the sentiments of pro-Clinton Democrats, and by extension to neoconservative foreign policy hawks. This was most apparent in the case of The Rachel Maddow Show (TRMS). A quantitative study conducted by *The Intercept* concerning all 28 TRMS episodes in the six-week period between February 20 and March 31 found that Russia-focused segments accounted for 53% of these broadcasts (Mate 2017). *Intercept* journalist Arron Mate (2017) points out that this figure is conservative, excluding segments where Russia was discussed, but was not the main topic. Maddow's pursuit of all things Russiagate was relentless. After Trump ordered a bombing operation in Syria in April 2017, gaining praise from virtually all major news outlets in the process, Maddow concurred with her co-anchor that Putin may have helped set the stage for the operation to boost Trump's domestic support. Apparently, Maddow's focus on Russia has paid off, with her ratings rising to their highest level since 2008 (Mate 2017).

Liberal Democrats were not the only constituency targeted by mainstream media outlets in the case of Russiagate. Certainly, it was inevitable that many right-wing news providers would rally to the President's defence, appealing to the populism and anti-elitism of his base. While most of the outlets in question are widely regarded as fringe media, one giant, FOX News, also attempted to cast doubt on the dominant narrative of Trump/Russia/WikiLeaks collusion. These efforts reached their peak in May 2017, when FOX's Sean Hannity chose to promote a particularly sensational conspiracy theory pertaining to Russiagate, one initially encouraged by Julian Assange. This concerned the notion that a 27-year-old, mid-level DNC staffer named Seth Rich had leaked the stolen emails, passing them on to WikiLeaks. In this version of reality, Rich was then murdered to prevent discovery of the leak's true origins. In addition to the attention it received on FOX, the story circulated rapidly within alternative forums online, was defended by Rush Limbaugh on his radio show and received coverage on RT. Newt Gingrich stated that the matter deserved further investigation, and even referred to Rich's death as an "assassination" (Dreyfuss 2017; Weigel 2017).

Seth Rich was indeed killed, having been shot twice in the back by an unknown assailant or assailants. The incident took place near his home in Northeast Washington on July 6, 2016. The DC police maintain that Rich was shot during a botched robbery attempt. Nothing was stolen from him, but there had been a string of recent robberies in the area, and bruises on Rich's hands and face showed signs of a struggle (Greenberg 2017; Weigel 2017). The conspiracy theory surrounding his death has received critical scrutiny in a range of publications and/or fact-checking websites including *The Nation*, *New York Magazine*, *Wired*, *Snopes* and *Media Matters*, and the various holes and problems identified in relation to it will not be reviewed here. For present purposes, it is enough to point out that on May 17, 2017 FOX News felt compelled to drop the story due to the absence of any hard evidence to back it up, even as Sean Hannity vowed to personally continue his investigation of the matter.

The incident stands out in large part because Assange had hinted that Rich might have been WikiLeaks' source for the DNC emails. During an interview on YouTube on Aug 9, 2016, Assange stated that "whistle-blowers go to significant efforts to get us material, and often take very significant risks. A 27-year-old, that works for the DNC, was shot in the back, murdered, just two weeks ago, for unknown reasons, as he was walking down the street in Washington" (Dreyfus 2017). When pressed by the interviewer as to whether he was suggesting a murder Assange stated further that "others have suggested that. We are investigating to understand what happened in the situation with Seth Rich". Shortly thereafter, WikiLeaks offered a $20,000 reward for information about the murder of Rich. Whether Assange himself truly believes, or once believed, that Seth Rich was the source of the alleged leak, or whether he was more interested in fuelling rumours that might gain WikiLeaks greater publicity—or perhaps some combination of the two—remains unclear. However, he continues to insist that the emails were not given to WikiLeaks by Russia, or any state source.

For the most part, and to much better effect, Assange has appeared less interested in provoking speculation as to how he obtained the DNC emails, opting instead to defend WikiLeaks' right to publish them in a manner consistent with the organization's long-standing claim to represent a new form of journalism. As he observed in an interview with Jeremy Scahill of *The Intercept*, WikiLeaks' decision to publish the DNC emails places it in essentially the same position as any other news organizations with an interest in this or similar stories. At one point, Scahill asks "if the documents were received from a foreign government, and you had verified the accuracy of them, the context of them, and that there wasn't some big missing piece, do you believe that those still should be published?" In response Assange answers affirmatively, and then quotes Dean Banquet, Editor of the *New York Times*, as follows:

> But I think that truth trumps strategy and everything else every day. And if a powerful figure writes emails that are newsworthy, you just gotta publish 'em. I mean, look, Edward Snowden stole documents. We, the Guardian, the Washington Post, and others reported them. I think they provoked one of the most compelling arguments about national security we've had in a generation. (Scahill 2017)

Returning to the case of FOX News, it may seem highly ironic that a reporter from the same organization whose "National Security Analyst" had once declared WikiLeaks a terrorist organization (see McFarland 2010) would court that same organization's leader as a respected news source. On January 3, 2017, Hannity even went so far as to travel to the Ecuadorian embassy in London to conduct a 90-minute exclusive interview with Assange for FOX. Some left-wing supporters of WikiLeaks clearly felt put off by the very fact of such an interview. Yet, as demonstrated in Chap. 5, Assange's willingness to cooperate with such diverse news operations as the *New York Times*, RT, *FOX News* and *Democracy Now*, while simultaneously providing a resource for countless smaller media forums and activists, is not inconsistent either with WikiLeaks' overall media strategy or with Assange's anarchist worldview. This was evident during an exchange taken from the same *Intercept* podcast cited above, which took place shortly after the Vault 7 disclosure. During the latter part of the interview, Jeremy Scahill presses Assange concerning the ethics of his exchanges with those supporting Donald Trump:

JS: I mean, just on a personal level, Julian, like, what was it like to see Trump citing WikiLeaks during the course of his campaign in the way that he did?

JA: Well, I mean, whenever a high-profile person cites our material, especially when a big audience is watching, we think, great, more people are gonna read it. From that perspective, we thought, well, this is great. Donald Trump is marketing our material. People are gonna read it.

JS: Yeah, but he got you some really reprehensible fans. I mean, come on, Sean Hannity comes over and sits down. I mean, Sean Hannity is an amoral charlatan.

JA: Yeah, but I don't—I'm not a groupist, if that makes sense.

JS: No, I know you're not, but come—give me a break. I mean, Sean Hannity is—he's a carnival barker for extreme rightwing causes in the United States, and he jumped onto the WikiLeaks bandwagon for his own partisan, narrow political purposes. He's no friend of WikiLeaks or free information.

JA: Yeah, and probably Sarah Palin did as well. But did Sarah Palin say the right thing? Did she do the right thing? Why, Sarah Palin said I should be hunted down like the Taliban. We published her emails in 2008, and she subsequently came out and apologized, and said that people should watch the Snowden film. So, this is very interesting. This is not just about WikiLeaks. This is about a, my guess, a certain perception amongst populist rightwing politicians like Sarah Palin, that the population has shifted in what it expects, and that critiques of mass surveillance and WikiLeaks are now something that are becoming something that's sayable. And of course, yes, on a particular—on the narrow basis, something that we publish which damages the reputation of Debbie Wasserman Schultz, the head of the DNC, or something like that—of course, that's just party political. But I wouldn't underestimate that there is an important transition in this populist right sphere. And you can talk about how it's been instrumentalized and so on. But there's a—I think a very important transition where a number of the grassroots on the populist right are saying wars or intervention are bad. The CIA is problematic. That's an extraordinary education that has occurred in that light. (Scahill 2017)

WikiLeaks does run the risk of being perceived as too closely associated with the agenda(s) of powerful domestic interests and/or of foreign powers in a manner that appears at odds with its self-proclaimed project of facilitating greater transparency and accountability on the part of dominant political and media institutions. Certainly, WikiLeaks' reputation would suffer were hard evidence to surface that Russia was indeed behind the DNC leak, thus exposing WikiLeaks as either naïve or dishonest and duplicitous in the process. The larger issue, however, concerns whether WikiLeaks will continue to have the opportunity to leak information that draws attention to systemic problems, such as those associated with global finance or the creeping powers of the security state, that transcend partisan politics and hold concern for a broad cross section of the public. Importantly in this regard, and despite insinuations from Hillary Clinton and others that some of the leaked DNC material may not be authentic, the group continues to be viewed as a reliable source of information even as it stands accused of aiding and abetting a foreign power. It deserves emphasis that the Jan 6, 2017, NIA states unambiguously that "disclosures through WikiLeaks did not contain any evident forgeries" (ODNI 2017). Notably, Russiagate did not prevent the subsequent Vault 7 leak from being treated as credible; it quickly became a major news story on virtually every American media network.

Insofar as commercial media organizations pursue the trend of targeting specific truth markets, or otherwise prove unable to resist sensationalizing the politically scandalous information that WikiLeaks periodically makes available, it will remain very difficult for these same organizations, and hence for politicians, to convincingly present WikiLeaks as a source of "fake news". Without doubt, Assange and the organization he leads will continue to be attacked or defended opportunistically by both mainstream and fringe actors oriented to various constituencies or truth markets, as dictated by the specifics of any given leak. Likewise, pundits like Sean Hannity and Rachel Maddow could easily swap positions overnight concerning the organization's character based on the next leak, accompanied by the requisite expressions of admiration/disgust concerning how WikiLeaks had suddenly lost/recovered its previous integrity/depravity. Over the long run such behaviour appears more likely to work in WikiLeaks' favour than against it, guaranteeing the activist platform's ongoing relevance while making its detractors appear inconsistent or hypocritical in the process.

There is, however, a larger related danger posed to WikiLeaks' capacity to function as an effective activist organization. As argued throughout this book, this concerns the ongoing possibility that any potentially valuable information the organization provides to the public will either be used selectively to reinforce dominant news narratives and/or lines of political propaganda or be diverted to feed the self-referential claims and counter-claims circulating amongst fragmenting truth markets in the manner described by Harsin (2015). The potential fallout in each case is essentially the same, namely, the trivialization or deflection of information that might otherwise lead to transformative grassroots action or constructive political reform. Throughout 2016–2017, both processes were visibly at work and frequently converged. The former dynamic played out to the extent that corruption within the DNC was sidelined by frenzied media attention to what is arguably a red herring, namely, the serious threat posed to American democracy by Russia. The latter process was observable in a related prolif-eration of unsubstantiated rumours and conspiracy theories, many of which were picked up by major news stations to better hold the attention of their target demographics. As the case of the Seth Rich conspiracy the-ory makes clear, WikiLeaks itself must exercise restraint if it hopes to pre-serve its integrity and avoid contributing to the negative trends in question.

Already there are signs that, for better or worse, recent events in which WikiLeaks has played a role may lead to further political change in the US. For example, commentators in both the mainstream and alternative media have speculated that mounting discontent with the political status quo may lead to splits within the Republican and/or the Democratic Parties or otherwise inspire reform. For example, Pollitt (2018) contends that while the Democrats continue to promote Russiagate, they are also attempting to acknowledge and deal with their problems. She points out that by March 2018 Democrats had won 40 state and legislative seats. Even more intriguing, the Democratic Socialists of America (DSA) have experienced an enormous surge of interest across the US. Since November 2016, the group's membership has increased from about 5000 to 35,000 nationwide, with the number of local groups growing from 40 to 181, including 10 in Texas (Stockman 2018). Likewise, many Democrats have begun to ask socialists for their support. Clearly, primary responsibility for such developments cannot be attributed to WikiLeaks. However, as with other groups involved in leaking the secrets of the powerful, it is undeni-able that the world's best-known whistle-blower platform has contributed to the increasing mistrust of dominant institutions that now represents a major driver of political change.

As argued in this and the previous chapter WikiLeaks' present media strategies appear well-suited, despite the hazards inherent in pursuing them, to a post-truth media environment. Crucially in this regard WikiLeaks' social/political influence, limited as it may be, does not hinge primarily on whether the organization or its leader are admired or despised by most Americans, or even whether most members of the public remain aware of the group's existence when it is not busy making news headlines. What is important is the growth and persistence of the political legitimation crisis to which the organization continues to contribute, even if only modestly, vis-à-vis the media forums and communication networks associated with major news organizations, web-based pundits and grassroots activists alike. The future evolution of the political and media environment that WikiLeaks must navigate is of course impossible to predict. Ultimately, whether the growing dissent in which WikiLeaks remains implicated leads to increasingly serious political crises in the US and elsewhere, or whether it is absorbed within the logic of communicative capitalism and its accompanying truth games, remains, as they say in newspeak, a developing story.

References

Binney, William, Skip Folden, Ed Loomis, Ray McGovern, and Kirk Wiebe. 2017. Why This Is Important. *The Nation*, September 1. https://www.thenation.com/article/a-leak-or-a-hack-a-forum-on-the-vips-memo/#vips-reply.

Boyd-Barrett, Oliver. 2004. Judith Miller, The New York Times, and the Propaganda Model. *Journalism Studies* 5 (40): 435–449. https://pdfs.semanticscholar.org/8ad5/37caa2dcca12dc5ad9415230a0d8b33f2e05.pdf.

Bratich, Jack Z. 2008. *Conspiracy Panics: Political Rationality and Popular Culture*. Albany: State University of New York Press.

Cassidy, John. 2016. Why Bernie Sanders Is Staying in the Race. *The New Yorker*, May 5. https://www.newyorker.com/news/john-cassidy/why-bernie-sanders-is-staying-in-the-race.

Confessore, Nicholas, and Steve Eder. 2016. In Hacked D.N.C. Emails, a Glimpse of How Big Money Works, *The New York Times*, July 25. https://www.nytimes.com/2016/07/26/us/politics/dnc-wikileaks-emails-fundraising.html?_r=0.

Dean, Jodi. 2002. *Publicity's Secret: How Technoculture Capitalizes on Democracy*. Ithaca/London: Cornell University Press.

Drake, Thomas, Scott Ritter, Lisa Ling, Cian Westmoreland, Philip M. Giraldi, and Jesselyn Radack. 2017. When Facts Are Not Facts. *The Nation*, September 1. https://www.thenation.com/article/a-leak-or-a-hack-a-forum-on-the-vips-memo/#vips-reply.

Dreyfus, Bob. 2017. Seth Rich, Conspiracy Theorists, and Russiagate 'Truthers'. *The Nation*, August 25. https://www.thenation.com/article/seth-rich-conspiracy-theorists-and-russiagate-truthers/.

Ellul, Jacques. 1965. *Propaganda: The Formation of Men's Attitudes*. New York: Vintage Books.

Gabriel, Trip. 2016. The More Donald Trump Defies His Party, the More His Supporters Cheer. *The New York Times*, February 17. https://www.nytimes.com/2016/02/18/us/politics/the-more-trump-defies-his-party-the-more-his-supporters-cheer.html.

Greenberg, John. 2017. Seth Rich: Separating Fact and Speculation. August 7. http://www.politifact.com/truth-o-meter/article/2017/aug/07/seth-rich-separating-fact-and-speculation/.

Greenwald, Glenn. 2017a. Yet Another Major Russia Story Falls Apart. Is Skepticism Permissible Yet? *The Intercept*, September 28. https://theintercept.com/2017/09/28/yet-another-major-russia-story-falls-apart-is-skepticism-permissible-yet/.

———. 2017b. The U.S. Media Suffered Its Most Humiliating Debacle in Ages and Now Refuses All Transparency Over What Happened. *The Intercept*, December 9. https://theintercept.com/2017/12/09/the-u-s-media-yesterday-suffered-its-most-humiliating-debacle-in-ages-now-refuses-all-transparency-over-what-happened/.

Haggerty, Kevin. 2005. Visible War: Surveillance, Speed, and Information War. In *The New Politics of Surveillance and Visibility*, ed. Kevin D. Haggerty and Richard V. Ericson, 251–267. Toronto: University of Toronto Press.

Harsin, Jayson. 2006. The Rumour Bomb: Theorising the Convergence of New and Old Trends in Mediated US Politics. *Southern Review: Communication, Politics and Culture* 39 (1): 84–110.

———. 2015. Regimes of Posttruth, Postpolitics, and Attention Economies. *Communication, Culture and Critique* ISSN: 1735–9129. http://onlinelibrary.wiley.com.libproxy.stfx.ca/doi/10.1111/cccr.12097/epdf.

Herman, Edward S. 2017. Fake News on Russia and Other Official Enemies: The New York Times, 1917–2017. *Monthly Review*, July–August. https://monthlyreview.org/2017/07/01/fake-news-on-russia-and-other-official-enemies/.

Heuvel, Katrina Vanden. 2017. Editor's Note. *The Nation*, August 9. https://www.thenation.com/article/a-new-report-raises-big-questions-about-last-years-dnc-hack/.

Johnson, Adam. 2016. Polls Showed Sanders Had a Better Shot of Beating Trump – But Pundits Told You to Ignore Them. *FAIR*, November 11. https://fair.org/home/polls-showed-sanders-had-a-better-shot-of-beating-trump-but-pundits-told-you-to-ignore-them/.

Kramer, Michael. 1996. Rescuing Boris: The Secret of How Four US Advisors Used Polls, Focus Groups, Negative Ads and All the Other Techniques of

American Campaigning to Help Boris Yeltsin Win. *Time*, July 15. https://ccisf.org/wp-content/uploads/2016/12/201612201405.pdf.

Lawrence, Patrick. 2017. A New Report Raises Big Questions About Last Year's DNC Hack. *The Nation*, August 9. https://www.thenation.com/article/a-new-report-raises-big-questions-about-last-years-dnc-hack/.

Marmura, Stephen. 2014. Likely and Unlikely Stories: Conspiracy Theories in an Age of Propaganda. *International Journal of Communication* 8: 2377–2395. http://ijoc.org/index.php/ijoc/article/viewFile/2358/1220.

Mate, Aaron. 2017. MSNBC's Rachel Maddow Sees a "Russia Connection" Lurking Around Every Corner. *The Intercept*, April 12. https://theintercept.com/2017/04/12/msnbcs-rachel-maddow-sees-a-russia-connection-lurking-around-every-corner/.

McChesney, Robert W. 2008. *The Political Economy of Media: Enduring Issues, Emerging Dilemmas*. New York: Monthly Review Press.

McFarland, Kathleen T. 2010. Yes, WikiLeaks Is a Terrorist Organization and the Time to Act Is Now. *FOX News*, November 30. http://www.foxnews.com/opinion/2010/11/30/yes-wikileaks-terrorist-organization-time-act.html.

Meyerson, Harold. 2016. Why Are There Suddenly Millions of Socialists in America? *The Guardian*, February 29. https://www.theguardian.com/commentisfree/2016/feb/29/why-are-there-suddenly-millions-of-socialists-in-america.

Naureckas, Jim. 2015. NYT Suggests Sanders Is 'Unelectable' for Siding with Majority on Tax Hikes for Rich. *FAIR*, July 1. https://fair.org/home/nyt-suggests-sanders-is-unelectable-for-siding-with-majority-on-tax-hikes-for-rich/.

Office of the Director of National Intelligence. 2017. Background to "Assessing Russian Activities and Intentions in Recent US Elections": The Analytic Process and Cyber Incident Attribution, January 6. https://www.dni.gov/files/documents/ICA_2017_01.pdf.

Parry, Robert. 2017. Russia-gate's Totalitarian Style. *Consortium News*, September 2. https://consortiumnews.com/2017/09/02/russia-gates-totalitarian-style/.

Patterson, John. 2016. Pre-Primary News Coverage of the 2016 Presidential Race: Trump's Rise, Sanders' Emergence, Clinton's Struggle. *Harvard Kennedy School: Shorenstein Center on Media, Politics and Public Policy*, June. https://shorensteincenter.org/pre-primary-news-coverage-2016-trump-clinton-sanders/.

Philo, Greg. 2007. Can Discourse Analysis Successfully Explain the Content of Media and Journalistic Practice? *Journalism Studies* 8 (2): 175–196. https://doi.org/10.1080/14616700601148804.

Pollitt, Katha. 2018. Let's Get Real About Russiagate. *The Nation*, March 8. https://www.thenation.com/article/lets-get-real-about-russiagate/.

Ritter, Scott. 2017. Russia-gate Report Ignored Iraq-WMD Lessons. *Consortium News*, July 16. https://consortiumnews.com/2017/07/16/russia-gate-report-ignored-iraq-wmd-lessons/.

Scahill, Jeremy. 2017. Intercepted Podcast: Julian Assange Speaks Out as Trump's CIA Director Threatens to "End" WikiLeaks. August 19. https://theintercept.com/2017/04/19/intercepted-podcast-julian-assange-speaks-out-as-trumps-cia-director-threatens-to-end-wikileaks/.

Shane, Scott. 2017. Russian Intervention in American Election Was No One-Off. *The New York Times*, January 6. https://www.nytimes.com/2017/01/06/us/politics/russian-hacking-election-intelligence.html.

Stockman, Farah. 2018. 'Yes, I'm Running as a Socialist.' Why Candidates Are Embracing the Label in 2018. *The New York Times*, April 20. https://www.nytimes.com/2018/04/20/us/dsa-socialism-candidates-midterms.html.

Taibbi, Matt. 2016. Something About This Russia Story Stinks. *Rolling Stone*, December 30. https://www.rollingstone.com/politics/features/something-about-this-russia-story-stinks-w458439.

Tufekci, Zeynep. 2016. Did You Hear the Latest About Hillary? *The New York Times*, September 12. https://www.nytimes.com/2016/09/13/opinion/campaign-stops/did-you-hear-the-latest-about-hillary.html.

Urchill, Joe. 2017. Why the Latest Theory About the DNC Not Being Hacked Is Probably Wrong. *The Hill*, August 14. http://thehill.com/policy/cybersecurity/346468-why-the-latest-theory-about-the-dnc-not-being-a-hack-is-probably-wrong.

Virilio, Paul, and Sylvere Lotringer. 1997. *Pure War.* New York: Autonomedia.

Walsh, Lucas, and Julien Barbara. 2006. Speed, International Security, and "New War" Coverage in Cyberspace. *Journal of Computer Mediated Communication* 12 (1): 189–208. https://doi.org/10.1111/j.1083-6101.2006.00321.x.

Weigel, David. 2017. The Life and Death of the Seth Rich Conspiracy Theory. *The Washington Post*, May 24. https://www.washingtonpost.com/powerpost/the-life-and-death-of-the-seth-rich-conspiracy-theory/2017/05/23/aba640c4-3ff3-11e7-adba-394ee67a7582_story.html?utm_term=.f72d4422d7fb.

WikiLeaks. 2017a. CIA Espionage Orders for the 2012 French Presidential Election. *WikiLeaks.org*, February 17. https://wikileaks.org/cia-france-elections-2012/.

———. 2017b. Vault 7: CIA Hacking Tools Revealed. *WikiLeaks.org*, March 7. https://wikileaks.org/ciav7p1/.

INDEX

© The Author(s) 2018
S. M. E. Marmura, *The WikiLeaks Paradigm*,
https://doi.org/10.1007/978-3-319-97139-1